2's Sensory Play EXPERIENCE

Look
　　Listen
　　　　Touch
　　　　　　Taste
　　　　　　　　Smell

2'S Sensory Play EXPERIENCE

by
Liz & Dick Wilmes

Illustrated by
Janet McDonnell

 **BUILDING BLOCKS Publication**

38W567 Brindlewood, Elgin, Illinois   60123

ART

Cover Design and Graphics: David VanDelinder
STUDIO 155
Elgin, Illinois 60123

Computer Graphics: Arlene Fiebig
PAPER PUSHERS
Darien, Wisconsin 53114

Text Graphics: Janet McDonnell
Early Childhood Artist
Arlington Heights, Illinois 60004

SPECIAL THANKS TO:

Cheryl Luppino and Mary Schuring for sharing so many multi-sensory games and activities for toddlers and twos to play each day.

PUBLISHED BY:

38W567 Brindlewood
Elgin, Illinois 60123

DISTRIBUTED BY:

Gryphon House	Consortium Book Sales	Monarch Books
P.O. Box 207	1045 Westgate Drive	5000 Dufferin St., Unit K
Beltsville, MD 20704	St. Paul, MN 55114	Downsview, Ontario
		Canada M3H 5T5
(Educational Stores & Catalogs)	*(U.S. Book Trade)*	*(All Canadian Orders)*

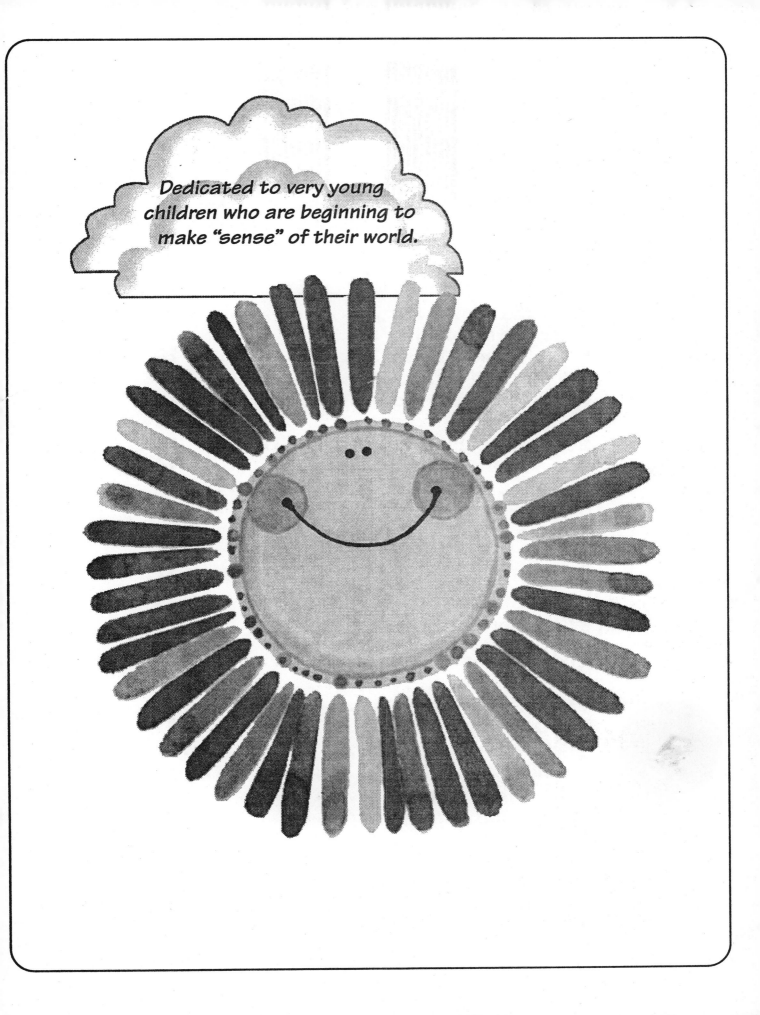

Dedicated to very young children who are beginning to make "sense" of their world.

Contents

Fun With Sounds

Fun With Sights

Fun With Foods

Fun With Smells

FUN WITH
WATER

WARM AND COLD TUBS

YOU'LL NEED

- Two rubber/plastic dish tubs
- Lots of ice cubes
- Warm water

PREPARATION

- Make 4-5 trays of ice cubes.

ACTIVITY

Put the two dish tubs in your empty water table. Put a little cold water in one tub. Have the children put on their smocks and help you carry several ice cube trays to the water table. Crack the ice trays. Give the children ice cubes and let them put the ice cubes in the tub with a little water. As they are doing this, talk about how the cubes feel.

After all the cubes are in one tub, fill the second tub about a quarter full with warm water. Let the children feel the water in both tubs by playing with it. As they play, talk about warm and cold.

MORE WARM AND COLD --

- **Touch:** Have several clean wash cloths or small towels. Dip one towel in the cold water. Gently press it on a child's wrist, palm of his hand, or cheek. *How does it feel?* Maybe a child would like to dip his fingers in the cold water and touch his own cheek. *How does it feel?* Do similar activities with the warm water.

AT THE BEACH

YOU'LL NEED

- Blue food coloring
- Sand
- Seashells
- Boats
- Water animals toys *(rubber squeezable animals are best.)*

PREPARATION

- Turn your water table into a BEACH:

  1. Put a little sand in the bottom.

  2. Add water and blue food coloring.

  3. Put the seashells, water animals, and boats in the water.

ACTIVITY

Have the children put on their smocks. Let them play with the beach toys in the water. Show the children how to help their water animals *"take drinks"* by squeezing them. Feel the seashells. *How do they feel -- hard, soft, bumpy, smooth, sharp, pointed, etc.?* Look at them. *Are there small ones? Are there big ones?*

HINT: Mix and match all the BEACH TOYS so children are encouraged to use them in a variety of ways.

MORE BEACH PLAY

Instead or in addition to the basic BEACH, you could have:

- Green craft grass for seaweed
- Rocks
- Pails and small scoops along with a little more sand and a little less water.

WATER

13

FROZEN SHAPE FUN

YOU'LL NEED

■ All types and sizes of molds

   - Plastic puzzle pieces which are very deep
     (animals, toys, people, vehicles, numbers, etc.)

   - Gelatin molds

   - Mini-ice cube trays

   - Shaped ice cube trays

■ Icicles in the winter

PREPARATION

■ Pour water into the molds and let it freeze overnight.

ACTIVITY

Fill your water table with a little water. Have the children put on their smocks and push up their sleeves. Let the children help you carry the ice molds to the water table. Crack each mold. Hand the ice shapes to the children and let them put the shapes in the water table.

Encourage the children to:

   - Look at the shapes. *What are they?*

   - Feel the shapes.

   - Watch the water in the water table. *What is happening to the ice shapes? What is happening to the water?*

MORE ICE MOLD PLAY

■ **Scoop and Drip:** Add slotted spoons. Let the children scoop the ice shapes onto the spoons and watch the water drip through the slots.

■ **Fill and Dump:** Add small buckets. Let the children fill the buckets with ice shapes and then dump them.

TOUCH THE TEDDY

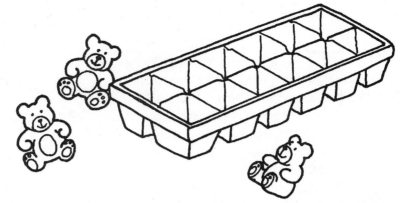

YOU'LL NEED

- Ice cube trays
- Teddy bear counters

PREPARATION

- Fill the ice cube trays with water. Put them in the freezer. When the water is partially hardened, put a teddy bear figure in each cube. Let the water completely harden.

ACTIVITY

Fill the water table with a little water. Have the children put on their smocks and help you carry the ice cube trays to the water table.

Break the cubes into the water. Play with the cubes. As you play watch the teddy bears. *Can you touch them?* Play some more. *What is happening?* After the ice cubes have melted, add some boats to the activity and let the children sail the teddy bears around.

OTHER TIMES: Freeze tiny dinosaurs, blocks, vehicles, plastic fruits, pegs, etc.

WATER

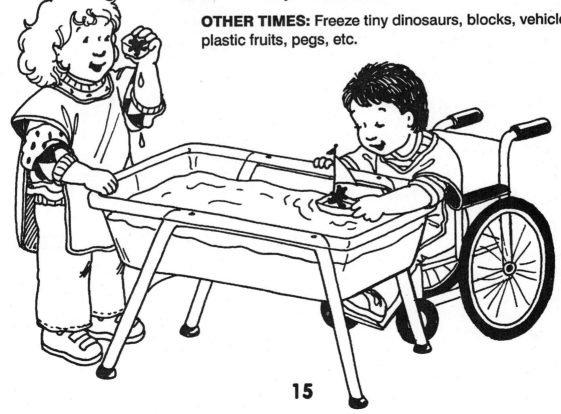

15

FUN WITH WATER TOYS*

PUMP BOTTLES -- *(Short, squat bottles like you get from the hair salons work well.)* Fill the bottles with water for the children. Put the bottles in the water table. Encourage the children to use the palms of their hands to pump the water into the water table. As each bottle is emptied, fill it again and let the children continue to play.

SMALL SPRINKLING CANS -- Fill the water table with a little water. Have scoops and measuring cups plus sprinkling cans. Let the children fill the sprinkling cans with as much water as each would like and then pour it out. Watch the water spray out of all the little holes.

Pour it over the children's hands and arms. *How does it feel? Does it tickle? Is it warm - cool?*

SIEVES -- Fill the water table with a little water. Have several different types of sieves each time you do this activity. Encourage the children to drag the sieves through the water, hold them up, and watch the water.

In addition to commercial sieves try some of these:

- Unbreakable flower pots with different size holes in the bottoms

- One and two liter soda bottles with holes punched in the bottoms and/or along the sides

- Large plastic cups with large holes punched in the bottoms

- All sizes of tea balls

WATER WHEEL -- Fill the water table with several inches of water. Put the water wheel in the table. Hold it steady and show the children how to make the wheel go around and around. Hold the wheel and let the children make it go around.

BASTERS -- Fill the water table with a little water. Have different size basters available. Let the children use the basters however they would like. As they play, show them how to suck up the water and then let it go. Encourage them to watch the water go up and down the baster.

CLEAR PLASTIC TUBES -- *(Get in plumbing section of hardware store - wide tubes best)* Fill the water table with a little clear water. Put several tubes in the water. Let the children use the tubes as they want. One of their favorite activities is to drag the tubes through the water.

Instead of playing with tubes in clear water, try these variations:

- Have colored water in the water table.

- Attach funnels to the tops of the plastic tubes. Have scoops. Let the children fill the funnels with water and then watch it "flood out" the bottoms of the tubes.

CLEAR SHAMPOO BOTTLE -- Fill the water table with a little water. Have small scoops and empty but not totally cleaned out shampoo bottles. Let the children fill, pour out, and refill the bottles as often as they'd like. It's great fun to watch the bubbles!

Lay the bottles on their sides. Watch them fill up. Dump them out - watch them fill up again.

❋Avoid cups because the children will use them to drink the water.

W
A
T
E
R

PAINT THE SNOW

YOU'LL NEED

- Several small pump-type spray bottles
- Food coloring
- Snow
- Mittens

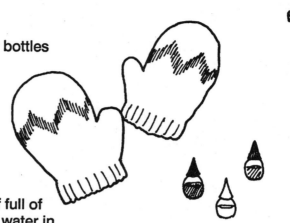

PREPARATION

- Fill each spray bottle about half full of water. Add food coloring to the water in each bottle.

ACTIVITY

Fill the water table with snow. Stick several spray bottles in the snow at each end of the water table.

When a child wants to paint, have her put on a smock and pair of mittens. Let her spray paint the snow as she wants. Have fun watching what is happening to the snow. *How does it look at first? How does it look with all the colors? What is happening as it melts?*

CLEAR WATER PAINTING

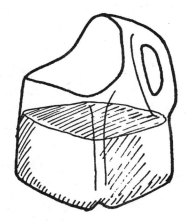
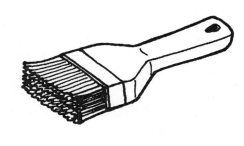

YOU'LL NEED

- House painting brushes
- Several lightweight pails
- Plastic milk bottles

PREPARATION

- Cut the milk bottles into buckets with handles. *(See illustration.)*

ACTIVITY

Help each child fill a bucket about half full of water. Give her a brush.

Let the children dip the brushes in the clear water and paint the building, playground equipment, concrete, grass, bushes, tree trunks, and benches for as long as each would like.

HINT: This is an especially good activity on a hot day.

- The water feels nice and cool on children's skin.
- Children also love to watch the water they've painted "disappear."

WATER

19

FUN WITH SNOW TOYS

HINT: Get a large mesh bag. *(Ask the produce manager at your local grocery store to save you several large potato sacks.)* Put your snow toys in it. Carry the bag to the activity and play. When you are finished put all the snow toys back in the bag. Put the whole bag in a sink so the snow can melt off and let the toys dry.

COOKIE CUTTERS -- *(Large cutters with easy grip handles work best.)* Let the children have the cutters they want and make shapes in the snow. Talk about what they have done.

MOLDS -- *(Gather molds which the child can easily grip, like individual gelatin molds. Remember, the children are wearing mittens and it is even more difficult for them to grasp things.)* Give children molds as they want them. Let them fill the molds with snow and turn them over. Other than molding, some children will probably fill and dump the snow -- others will cut into the snow -- still others may drag the molds along making snow trails.

Play **Mold and Smash** -- Use the molds to build "snow castles." Let the children take their mittened hands and smash down the "castles" you've built. Do over and over. Children love it.

HOES AND PLASTIC RAKES -- Have lots of rakes and hoes. When you are outside give them to the children to rake and drag snow around. Have them look at the trails they are making in the snow.

BUCKET OF STICKS OR DOWEL RODS -- Take the bucket outside. Help the children build "birthday cakes" in the snow and use the sticks/rods for candles. Sing *Happy Birthday* over and over. "Eat" the cake and then bake another one. Add the candles.

SAND PAILS AND SHOVELS -- Sit with the children and fill up the pails with snow and then dump them.

DIG FOR DINOSAURS

YOU'LL NEED

- Dinosaur counters
- Snow
- Mittens
- Plastic container

PREPARATION

- Put dinosaurs in a bucket.

**W
A
T
E
R**

ACTIVITY

Fill the water table with snow. Have the children put on smocks, push up their sleeves, and slip on mittens.

Give each child a dinosaur and tell him to bury it deep in the snow. Continue letting the children bury the dinosaurs until they are all in the snow. Look at the snow. "*Does anyone see a dinosaur?*" Have the children reach into the snow and dig around until they feel dinosaurs. Whenever a child feels one, have him pull it out and put it back into the container. Keep digging for the dinosaurs until the children think they have found them all.

Let the children bury and find the dinosaurs as long as they want.

HINT: Some children may prefer to find dinosaurs and bury them again right away -- this is a little less structured.

21

FUN WITH OUTSIDE WATER TOYS

SQUIRT BOTTLES -- Get several squirt bottles with trigger-type handles. Fill them about half full of water. Let the children squirt the buildings, bushes, concrete, and playground equipment. Watch the water. Does it disappear?

SOAKER-TYPE HOSES -- Hook up the hose to your outside faucet. Lay it along the building so that it is out of the general traffic. Turn the water on so that it bubbles up several inches. Have the children take off their shoes and socks and walk along it. *How does the water feel? Does it "tickle?"*

HINTS:

■ Some children may be apprehensive of the water coming out the hoses. Hold their hands when they are first trying the hose activities.

■ Create a "safe" area. Have beach blankets and several children's lawn chairs near the hose for the children who want to be close to the water, but not actually in it. Here children can participate in the play by watching the others.

NOZZLE-TYPE HOSES -- Hook up
a hose to your outside faucet. Turn it on so
the water trickles out the nozzle. Let the
children take off their shoes and socks and
enjoy the "feel" of the cool, refreshing water
on their feet and hands.

WATER TROUGH -- Hook the
hose to the trough. Let the children help
you fill it about half full of water. Add
some boats and/or other water toys. Let
the children play.

Before you go in, have the children help
you drain the water so that the trough is
ready to fill another time. It is as much fun
to watch the water drain to the ground as
it is to watch the trough fill up.

W A T E R

BUBBALOONS AND BUBBLE
MACHINES -- Create lots and lots of
giant bubbles for children to chase, catch,
and smash. Talk about how many bubbles
the children see. *What happens to the
bubbles? Where do they go?*

DO THE LAUNDRY

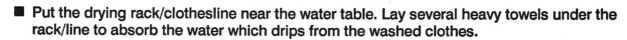

YOU'LL NEED

- Drying rack/clothesline
- Heavy towels
- Doll clothes/infant clothes
- Clothespins

PREPARATION

- Put the drying rack/clothesline near the water table. Lay several heavy towels under the rack/line to absorb the water which drips from the washed clothes.

- Put the clothespins in a bag. Hang the bag on the drying rack/line.

ACTIVITY

Fill the water table with a little bit of warm water. Have the children put on their smocks.

Let them wash the baby clothes in the water table. After the clothing is washed, have the children squeeze out each piece before hanging it on the drying rack/clothesline. *(If necessary, show the children how to use the clothespins.)*

As the children are washing clothes, talk with them about how they get their clothes dirty. *Do they play in the mud? Do they wipe dirty hands on their pants and shirts?* Have them look at the clothes they are wearing. *Are they dirty? How did they get dirty?*

HINT: Keep the water table filled with a little water.

BATHE THE BABIES

YOU'LL NEED

- Baby bubble bath
- Towels
- Empty powder containers
- Baby blankets
- Doll babies
- Wash cloths

PREPARATION

- Put a little warm water and bubble bath in your water table.
- Put a small table near the water table. Set the towels, powder, and baby blankets on it.

ACTIVITY

Have the children put on their smocks. When they want to give the babies baths, hand them dolls and wash cloths. Let them wash the babies for as long as they would like. Remind the children to be careful of the babies' eyes. After each baby is clean, encourage the child to dry off the baby, powder him, and wrap him tightly in a blanket.

While the children are bathing their babies, talk with the children about their own baths. *Do they like to take baths in warm or cold water? Do they play in the bath tub? How? With toys? What toys? How does the big warm towel feel after getting out of the water?*

MORE BABY PLAY

- **Rock the Babies:** Put the rocking boat or a rocking chair nearby. Encourage the children to sing to the babies after their baths.

W A T E R

SPRINKLER DAY

YOU'LL NEED

- Bathing suits
- Swim shoes
- Beach towels
- Several lawn chairs

- Several types of sprinklers
  - Soaker sprinklers that are flush with the ground
  - One direction sprinklers -- not the type that moves back and forth (*too difficult for children to judge where the water is.*)

PREPARATION

- Send a note home to families to let them know what day is SPRINKLER DAY. Tell them what (*if anything*) to send to school that day, such as bathing suits, swim shoes, and/or towels.

ACTIVITY

Have the children put on their bathing suits and swim shoes. Lay the beach towels on the ground. Set up the lawn chairs. Lay the sprinklers on the ground and hook them to the hoses and faucets.

Let the children enjoy the water spraying out of the sprinkler. *How does it feel?*

HINTS:

- When you start the sprinklers, spray them on a low setting until the children get used to the direction and feel of spraying water. Gradually increase the intensity.

- Have adults walk with children through the sprinkler until they become comfortable with spraying water.

WASH THE DISHES

YOU'LL NEED

- Two dish tubs
- Liquid dish soap
- Lots of small sponges
- Disposable wipes
- Scrub brushes
- Drying towels

- Lots of unbreakable dishes, pots, cooking utensils, and tableware
  - Plates
  - Bowls
  - Cups
  - Mixing spoons
  - Spatulas
  - Saucepans

PREPARATION

- Cut the sponges and wipes into small pieces. *(The children need small pieces so the washing process does not become too cumbersome.)*

- Set a small table next to the water table. Put the drying towels and "dirty dishes" on it.

ACTIVITY

Have the children put on their smocks. Put two dish tubs in the water table. Pour a little warm water into each one. Add dish detergent. Let the children mix the water and soap around. Talk about the bubbles. Put several sponges and scrub brushes in each tub.

Let the children take the "dirty dishes" off the table, put them in the dish tubs, and wash them. When finished, dry them and put them back on the table. Talk with the children about how the dirty dishes look at their house, after lunch at school, etc. *How do the dishes look after they've been washed? Do they help wash dishes at home?*

WATER

SOAPY WATER FUN

YOU'LL NEED

■ Liquid dish soap

PREPARATION

■ Put a little water in the water table. Add dish soap. Have the children put on their smocks and stir the soap and water around until it is bubbly.

ACTIVITY

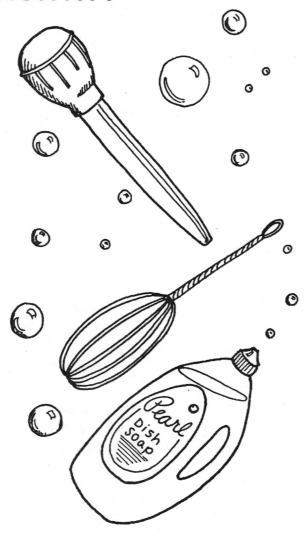

MAKE BUBBLES

■ **Turkey Basters:** Get several different sizes of turkey basters. Show the children how to squeeze the rubber ball at the top of each one. Let the children make bubbles by squeezing the basters in the water. Watch the bubbles. *Are they big? Little? Lots of them? Just a few? Piles of bubbles?*

LISTEN! Can you hear the air suck up and squeeze out the bubbles?

■ **Wire Whisks:** Get different sizes of wire whisks. Let the children whip the water and soap. *What happens? Where are the bubbles? Can you make lots of bubbles?*

■ **Dish Soap Bottles:** Have lots of "almost empty" dish soap bottles. Let the children squeeze the bottles in the water and watch the bubbles come out.

SMASH BUBBLES

- **Hands:** Have the children use their hands to smash the bubbles in the water table. Encourage the children to watch the bubbles as they smash them. *Can they feel the bubbles?*

- **Unbreakable Plates:** Have unbreakable plastic plates. Have the children lay the plates over the bubbles and smash them down. *Watch the bubbles! Did they disappear?*

CAPTURE BUBBLES

- **Strawberry Cartons, Small Sieves, Slotted Spoons:** Make lots of bubble water with the children. Let them use different things to "capture" the bubbles in. *Look -- How many bubbles did you catch?* Catch some more! *What do the bubbles look like?* Shh. Put them up to your ear. *Do they make noise?* Smell them. *Do they smell good? Not so good?*

- **Hands:** Make lots of bubbly water with the children. Have them use one or two hands to capture bubbles. *Can they feel the water and the bubbles? How do the bubbles feel? Are the bubbles popping --* keep watching *-- did they disappear?*

WATER

COLORED ICE EGGS

YOU'LL NEED

- Large plastic eggs
- Styrofoam egg cartons
- Food coloring

PREPARATION

- Divide each plastic egg in half. Put each half into a section of the egg carton. Fill each egg-half about 3/4 full of water. Add a little food coloring to the water in each egg-half. Stir a little to mix the coloring. Freeze the colored water.

ACTIVITY

Fill the water table with a little water. Have the children put on their smocks and help you carry the egg cartons with the plastic eggs to the water table.

Have the children help you put all the eggs in the water. Begin playing. Soon the colored eggs will come loose from the plastic molds. Keep playing. *What colors are the eggs? What is happening to the water in the water table? What is happening to the eggs? Do they feel cold?*

ICE POPSICLE PAINTING

YOU'LL NEED

- Butcher paper
- Dry tempera paint
- Ice cube trays
- Popsicle sticks

PREPARATION

- Cut the butcher paper to fit in your water table or messy trays.

- Make the ICE POPSICLES. Fill several ice cube trays with water. When the cubes are partially hardened, put a popsicle stick at a slight angle in each one. Let them completely harden.

- Pour dry tempera paint into shaker bottles.

ACTIVITY

Lay the paper in your table/trays. Pop out several popsicles and put them in a pie pan. Have the children put on their smocks and push up their sleeves.

Sprinkle several colors of paint on the paper. Let the children use the popsicles to smear the paint around the paper. Sprinkle more paint and let the children continue to smear it. When finished, hang the colored mural. Put another paper in the table/tray and paint some more.

On A Warm Day: Take this activity outside and set it up on a table. Hang the finished murals on the fence.

FUN WITH SQUISH BAGS

YOU'LL NEED

- SEAL-A-MEAL® machine and plastic bags *(large discount stores)*
- Variety of "things" to push around with fingers

    - Media Mix® and glitter
    - Corn starch and water mixture (GOOP)
    - White glue and food coloring
    - Soft dough or clay
    - Fingerpaint such as commercial paint, paste and food coloring, shaving gel, dual-colored toothpaste

- Variety of "things" to shake and watch

    - Glitter in clear water
    - Sand mixed with dry tempera paint
    - Buttons in vegetable oil
    - Dish soap in water
    - Mineral oil, food coloring, and water

- Variety of "things" to shake and listen

    - Bells
    - Sand
    - Buttons
    - Craft grass
    - Sawdust

PREPARATION

(Make lots of different SQUISH BAGS -- You can hardly have too many.)

- Make SQUISH BAGS

    1. Decide which "thing" or combination of "things" you want in each SQUISH BAG.
    2. Cut plastic the size you want. Make each one a double thickness. Follow the directions on the SEAL-A-MEAL® box and seal each SQUISH BAG.

ACTIVITY

Put all the SQUISH BAGS in a dish tub. Put the tub on a shelf so it is within easy, quick reach. Let the children use the BAGS all the time. Simply bring the tub down and set it on the floor/table. Give each child a BAG and let her play with it for as long as she wants and then trade it for another one.

Children will:

- Squish them

- Pound them

- Shake them

- Slide them between their fingers

- Press them between their hands

- Smear the ingredients around the bag

- Poke them

- Listen to them

- Look at them

- LOTS -- LOTS MORE.

MORE SQUISH BAG FUN

■ **Floating Fish:** Get flat plastic fish and other water animals. Put the fish with blue water in the bag.

■ **Jiggling Ice Cubes:** Float colored ice cubes in clear water in the bag.

■ **Fill and Dump:** Put small SQUISH BAGS in empty baby wipe boxes. Put the boxes on the floor. Let the children dump the BAGS out, stuff them back into the container and dump again.

FUN WITH TEXTURE

CUDDLY BOXES

YOU'LL NEED

- Sturdy cardboard boxes big enough for one child to comfortably sit in

- Several different pieces of soft fabric

PREPARATION

- Make the CUDDLY BOXES
  (for each box)

1. Measure the sides and bottom of the box.

2. Cut the fabric to fit on each side/bottom.

3. Glue the fabric to the inside of the box.

4. Repeat for each CUDDLY BOX.

ACTIVITY

Put the CUDDLY BOXES in different areas of the classroom, and let the children sit in them and do different activities, such as:

- Look at picture books.

- Build with small blocks.

- Drive cars and other vehicles.

- Talk to a stuffed animal.

- Take a rest.

BLOCK PLAY

YOU'LL NEED

- 2 messy trays or commercial sheet cake pans
- Variety of blocks
  - Wooden
  - Fabric
  - Cardboard
  - Bristle
  - Foam
  - Plastic

PREPARATION

- None

ACTIVITY

Put the messy trays on a large table. Lay the blocks on the trays. Let the children play. They might arrange the blocks end-to-end, stack them, or build very simple structures. While they are playing, encourage the children to feel the blocks they are holding. Ask children to squeeze their blocks -- *Do they feel hard? Soft? Squishy?* Have the children rub the blocks on their arms. *Do they feel rough? Smooth?*

MORE BLOCK PLAY

- **Stack and Crash:** Have the children stack the blocks and then knock them over. *How did they sound when they fell?*

- **On the Floor:** Have all the blocks in a big box. Set it on the floor. Let the children dump out the blocks and play with them as they wish.

TEXTURES

PEEK-A-BOO ANIMAL FOLDERS

YOU'LL NEED

- Old file folders
- Several large metal binder rings
- Picture of a fish, duck, sheep, mouse, and bear (*or use the patterns*)
- Textures for each animal
    - Sequined bric-brac for fish
    - Feathers for duck
    - Cotton for sheep
    - Fake fur fabric for mouse
    - Corduroy for bear

PREPARATION

- Make the PEEK-A-BOO ANIMAL FOLDERS

1. Have all the animal pictures. Glue a texture on a portion of each animal. For example, the furry fabric on the mouse's tail, the feathers on the duck's head, the cotton on the sheep's back, etc.

2. Cut the file folders horizontally in half or thirds depending on the size of the animal picture you are going to glue on each one.

3. Open each cut-down folder. Glue a textured animal to the inside right hand page of each small folder.

4. Close the folders. Make a pencil dot on each outside page to mark where the texture of the animal is. Cut a hole in the outside page to reveal a portion of the texture. Close the folder.

5. Punch a hole in the upper left hand corner of each folder. Slip them all on a ring binder.

6. Make several sets of books -- either more animals or pick other categories such as people. Use different fabrics on people's clothes.

ACTIVITY

Put all the PEEK-A-BOO FOLDERS in a big tub. Set the tub high on a shelf so it is within quick, easy reach.

Put the tub on a table or floor. Pass out the books to the children *(one for each)*. Let them feel the textures and then open the folders to see what is hiding inside. *What is it?* Name it. Continue encouraging the children to feel the textures and peek at the animals inside. After awhile maybe the children will want to guess what the pictures are before they peek at them.

PLAY ANIMAL SOUNDS

Have the children feel the textures with the folders closed. As the children are peeking at the animals inside, make the animals' sounds with them. Listen to the sounds. *Do the animals make loud sounds? Soft sounds? Squeaky ones? Rough, growling ones? Friendly ones?*

Quack, quack!

41

EGG CARTON SIDEWALK

YOU'LL NEED

- Lots of dozen and a half cardboard egg cartons
- Wide tape
- One side of a refrigerator appliance box

PREPARATION

- Make the EGG CARTON SIDEWALK

  1. Open up all the egg cartons. Lay them end-to-end along the cardboard.
  2. Tape the egg cartons down around the entire outside edge. Tape the cartons themselves together if necessary.

ACTIVITY

Lay the EGG CARTON SIDEWALK on the floor in an open area of the room. Have the children take off their shoes and walk along the path. *How do the egg cartons feel?* Some children might like to walk along the path with their socks off also. Let them. *How do bare feet feel on the EGG CARTON SIDEWALK?* Have the children be very quiet. *Can they hear the egg cartons squishing under their feet?* Walk slowly. *Can they hear the egg cartons now?*

STICKY WALK

YOU'LL NEED

■ Adhesive paper

PREPARATION

■ Prepare the STICKY WALK:

1. Cut a long piece of adhesive paper.
2. Bring it to an open area of the room. Remove the backing paper.
3. Securely tape the adhesive paper, sticky side up, to the floor.

ACTIVITY

Have the children take off their shoes and walk on the sticky paper. *Is it hard to walk on the sticky paper? How does it feel?* After they get used to the *"feel"* of the paper, encourage them to move in different ways - tiptoe, crawl, march, scoot, etc.

When finished, help each child put her shoes back on.

HINTS:

■ If any child is a little apprehensive about the activity, hold his hand as he walks on the paper.

■ You could also take off your shoes and walk hand-in-hand with him on the paper.

TEXTURES

OUTSIDE TEXTURE MAZE

YOU'LL NEED

- Watered-down white tempera paint
- Empty spray bottles

PREPARATION

- Make the OUTSIDE MAZE *(Do this after the children have left or before they come.)*

  1. Look at your outside play area. Find all the textures on the ground -- concrete, dirt, sand, grass, water, wood, etc.

  2. Lay out a simple path so the children will walk on all the textures your area offers.

  3. Pour the white paint in a spray bottle, and lightly spray a line along the path you've created. About two feet from the first line, spray a second line parallel to it. You have created the maze or path the children can walk along.

ACTIVITY

As soon as you go outside show the children the special path you've created for them. Take a walk along the path with all those who would like to go.

During the outside time, have the children take off their shoes and socks and walk barefoot along the TEXTURE MAZE. *Did the grass tickle? Is anything hard to walk on? Soft? Did anything cover their feet? What scratched their feet? What did they see along their walk? Dandelions?* Stop along the way and listen for sounds. *What do you hear?*

ANOTHER TIME: Let the children crawl along the maze like tigers. *How does the (grass) feel on their paws? How do the tigers sound?*

HINT: Though you can offer this activity any time, it is especially good when children already have their shoes/socks off such as during water activities.

Roaar!

TAKE A TEXTURE WALK

YOU'LL NEED

- Refrigerator or large appliance box
- Large pieces of different textures, such as

    - Fake fur
    - Sandpaper
    - Astro turf
    - Foam padding
    - Shag carpeting
    - Corrugated cardboard
    - Bath mat
    - Cotton batting
    - Bubble pack

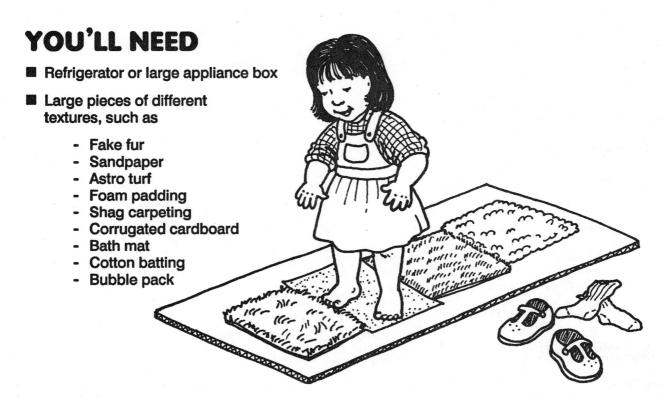

PREPARATION

- Make the TEXTURE WALK

1. Cut off one side of the appliance box and lay it on the floor. *(Cut up the rest of the cardboard for other activities.)*
2. Lay the textures on the cardboard, so they touch each other, creating a path. Glue them to the cardboard.

ACTIVITY

Lay the TEXTURE WALK on the floor in an open area of your room. Have the children take off their shoes and socks and walk along the path. Hold children's hands if they would like. *What tickles their feet? Anything feel squishy? What does the sandpaper feel like on their toes? Shhh! Listen. Can they hear any noises as they walk along?*

HINT: This is a great activity any time, but especially good when the children already have their shoes/socks off such as when they are playing "shoe store" or outside when you have the hose set up.

T
E
X
T
U
R
E
S

GUESS WHAT'S IN MY POCKET

YOU'LL NEED

- Apron with at least one pocket
- Small objects, such as:
    - Unsharpened pencil
    - Ball
    - Block
    - Doll
    - Cup
    - Spoon

PREPARATION

- None

ACTIVITY

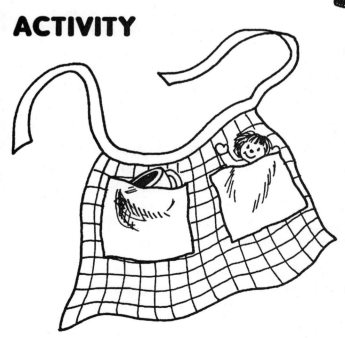

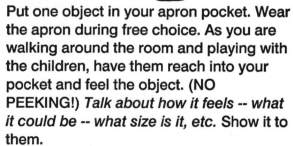

Put one object in your apron pocket. Wear the apron during free choice. As you are walking around the room and playing with the children, have them reach into your pocket and feel the object. (NO PEEKING!) *Talk about how it feels -- what it could be -- what size is it, etc.* Show it to them.

ANOTHER TIME: On another day wear the apron to group time. Walk around and let the children feel the object. Talk about it. Then slowly take the object out of your pocket, keeping it cupped in your hand. Straighten out your arm. Slowly uncup your hand so all the children can see the object. Pass it around and let the children feel it.

TEXTURE BAG

YOU'LL NEED

- Large paper or cloth bag

- All types of textures *(enough for each child -- several of each one)*

  - Infants' texture balls

  - Craft feathers

  - Silk fabric pieces

  - Sandpaper pieces

  - Large pompons

  - Gourds with bumpy surfaces

  - Balls that squeak when you squeeze them

PREPARATION

- Put all the textures in the TEXTURE BAG

ACTIVITY

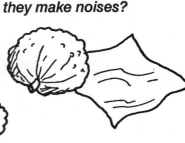

Sit on the floor with the children. Slowly open up the TEXTURE BAG. Hand several children one type of texture, such as the gourds. Encourage them to feel the gourds, slowly rolling them on their hands and arms. *How do they feel?* While these children are feeling their gourds, hand out another texture to several other children. *(Do this quickly, because all the children are anxious to have a texture.)* Encourage them to begin feeling their textures. Continue in this way until all the children are feeling textures.

As you play, have the children exchange textures. Talk about how each one feels. Show the children how to rub two textures together, such as the sandpaper or gourds. *How do they sound?* Try to squeeze some of the textures. *What happens? How do they feel? Do they make noises?*

TEXTURES

47

PULL-OUTS

YOU'LL NEED

- 4-5 tall, boutique-type tissue boxes
- Variety of fabric such as:
    - flannel
    - silk
    - cotton
    - burlap

  (enough to fill the tissue boxes)
- Wide tape

PREPARATION

- Reinforce the opening of each tissue box

ACTIVITY

Place the PULL-OUTS on a messy tray and put it on one of your tables. Let the children pull out the fabrics and stuff them back in their boxes. As they are *"pulling and stuffing"* talk about how the different fabrics feel. The children may want to rub the fabrics on their cheeks or arms. Switch the textures around and stuff different ones into the boxes.

Let your voice get very quiet. Tell the children to listen as they pull the fabric from the boxes. *Can they hear the fabric coming out? Is it scrapping on the opening? Which fabrics make loud sounds? Quiet sounds? No sounds?*

BABY LOTION MASSAGE

YOU'LL NEED

■ Baby lotion ✱

PREPARATION

■ None

ACTIVITY

Sit or kneel on the floor with the children. Have them hold out their hands. Gently hold each child's hand so the backside faces up. Squirt a small dab of lotion on it. (*Do this for each child.*)

Let each child rub the lotion on his hand, cheeks, arms, nose, etc. Go slowly, talk quietly. This is a very soothing, gentle activity.

MORE BODY LOTION MASSAGES

■ **Know Your Body Parts:** Quietly sing THIS IS THE WAY WE RUB OUR FACE as the children are rubbing lotion on different parts of their bodies.

THIS IS THE WAY WE RUB OUR FACE
(tune: This Is the Way We Wash Our Clothes)

This is the way we rub our face
Rub our face, rub our face.
This is the way we rub our face
So early every day.

♦ *Arms*   ♦ *Legs*
♦ *Knees*   ♦ *Fingers*

✱ Check your allergy list to be sure that none of the children are allergic to the baby lotion you are using.

TEXTURES

49

TEXTURE MITTENS

YOU'LL NEED

- Dish tub
- Lots of used young children's mittens
- Spray glue or watered-down white glue

- Variety of textures, such as:
  - Different fabrics
    (leather, silk, fake fur, flannel, backside of sweatshirts, etc.)
  - Sandpaper
  - Foam rubber
  - Textured wallpaper
  - Corrugated cardboard

PREPARATION

- Make the TEXTURE MITTENS

  1. Cut the textures to fit on the upper half of the fronts and backsides of the mittens.

  2. Put the textures in pairs so that each pair has two distinct "feels" such as a piece of sandpaper and a piece of silk would be rough and smooth, the foam rubber and leather would squishy and hard, and so on.

  3. Lay the mittens in a row. Put one pair of textures with each mitten. Glue one texture on the upper half front of each mitten and the other one on the upper half backside of each mitten. Let them dry.

- Put the TEXTURE MITTENS in the dish tub.

ACTIVITY

front

back

Set the tub of TEXTURE MITTENS on a high shelf so that it is readily available during the day.

Put the tub on the floor. Hand each child a mitten. Have her put it on and feel the textures on both sides. *Do they feel the same? Different?* Then encourage the children to rub their mittens on their knees, cheeks, and arms. *How do the textures feel? Are any scratchy? Do any tickle? Are any so soft?* Switch mittens and continue to play. Talk about how the textures feel.

MORE TEXTURE MITTEN PLAY

- **Noisy Textures:** Have the children put on 2 mittens and rub the textures together. *What do they sound like? Which textures make loud noises? Soft noises? No noises?*

GIANT TEXTURE BOARD

YOU'LL NEED

- Large appliance box
- Heavy duty string
- Wide variety of textures
    - Bath mat
    - Pegboard
    - Carpet squares
    - Fake fur fabric
    - Styrofoam
    - Foam rubber
    - Sandpaper

PREPARATION

- Make the TEXTURE BOARD

1. Cut off one side of the appliance box.

2. Cut large pieces of each texture.

3. Lay the different textures on the cardboard. Trim the textures that don't fit quite right.

4. Hot-glue the textures to the board.

5. Punch 4 holes along the top edge of the board.

6. Tie the heavy-duty string in each hole.

7. Hang the TEXTURE BOARD on a hallway or classroom wall, so that it lands within the children's easy reach.

ACTIVITY

Throughout the day let children touch the TEXTURE BOARD as they walk by it. Talk about it as they touch it. *What are they touching? Do they have anything at home that feels like it? How does it feel?* If they are touching something bumpy like the bath mat, you could ask them to touch the pegboard. *Does it feel bumpy too?*

TEXTURES

FINGER PAINTING

YOU'LL NEED

- Different types of "finger paint":
    - Commercial
    - Mud
    - Flour and water mixture
    - Liquid starch
    - Shave cream

- Different types of surfaces to paint on:
    - Shower mats
    - Door mats
    - Cookie sheets
    - Oilcloth
    - Bubble pack
    - Large pieces of pegboard
    - Tile

PREPARATION

- Choose one surface and one type of "finger paint" you want the children to use.

- Put the "finger paint" in an appropriate container. For example the liquid starch and flour-water mixture are runny and best in squeeze bottles, while the mud and commercial paint are thick enough to be spooned from margarine containers.

ACTIVITY

Tape the surface you've chosen to the art table. Put the finger paint containers nearby. Have smocks for the children to wear.

When children want to finger paint have them put on smocks and push up their sleeves. Squirt/spoon finger paint onto the surface and let the children paint for as long as they want. *Look at your fingers. They sure have lots of finger paint on them. How does the finger paint feel?*

FIND FARM ANIMALS

YOU'LL NEED

- Craft grass or straw
- Lots of small plastic/rubber farm animals
- Shoe box

PREPARATION

- Fill the water table with craft grass/straw.
- Put the animals in a shoe box.

Mooo!

TEXTURES

ACTIVITY

Bring the shoe box to the water table. Give each child an animal. Have him hide it in the grass/straw. Keep giving the children animals until they are all hidden. *Does the grass/straw feel scratchy?* Put the empty shoe box in the middle of the water table.

Now encourage the children to feel around the grass/straw and find the animals. When they find each one, make its sound and put it in the box/barn. Keep looking and making lots of animal sounds. Comment on the animal sounds. For example *"Wow, Mary! You are making very loud cow sounds." "Let's listen to Cheryl's pig sound."*

TEXTURES IN THE WATER TABLE

YOU'LL NEED

- Acorns
- Pine cones
- Bird seed
- Cotton balls
- Fresh grass
- Leaves
- Dirt/mud
- Papier maché
- Sand
- Shaving cream
- Shredded paper
- Snow
- Tubs of warm and cold water
- Large ice cubes

PREPARATION

- Decide what medium you are going to put in the water table. Gather as much as you need. Put it in the table or in dish tubs which are then set in the water table.

ACTIVITY

Let the children play with the medium you put in the table. If needed add a minimal amount of props to help the children become involved with the activity. You really want the children to touch and feel the medium.

Dirt - Sand: Encourage the children to "dig" with their hands. *How does the dirt/sand feel? Smell?* Look for lumps in the dirt. Have the children crumble them with their fingers.

Acorns: Have different size containers that the children can fill and dump. Let them use their hands for "shovels."

Pine Cones: Have different sizes and types of cones in the table. Compare how they feel and look. Ask children to find the small ones. Giant ones. Fat ones. Tall ones. Give them to you to hold. Talk a little as each child hands you her acorn.

Bird Seed: Have several different containers that sound very different when you pour the seed into them *(styrofoam plate, metal pail, wooden box, margarine tub)*. Let the children use their hands for "shovels." Encourage them to watch the seed pour out of their hands. *Do they see any dust? Look carefully. Is the seed pouring slowly? Quickly?* Listen. *How does the seed sound when it hits the container?*

Cotton Balls: Have margarine tubs with the cotton balls. Let the children fill and dump the containers. *Do they hear any sounds?* Encourage them to rub the cotton on their cheeks and arms. *How does it feel?*

Fresh Grass Clippings: Have very small rakes in the water table. As the children are "raking" encourage them to smell the grass. After several days, take a good look at it. *Do the children see any brown grass?* Feel it. *Does it feel like the green grass?*

Colored Leaves: Let the children play with the leaves. As they are playing talk about the colors and sizes. Look for specific colors or sizes of leaves. *Here is a giant leaf. Let's find more big ones.*

Dried Leaves: Encourage the children to smash and squish the leaves. *How do they sound? Do they smell?* Find the stems in the pile of leaves. Put them in a margarine tub. Keep looking. The more you smash the leaves, the more stems will appear.

Shaving Cream: Squirt as much shaving cream in the water tub as you want. Have the children put on their smocks and play.

Shredded Paper: Fill the table with shredded paper. Encourage the children to dig into it, tear it, rustle it, and so on. *How does it sound?*

TEXTURES

SILLY PUTTY

YOU'LL NEED

- White glue
- Liquid starch (Sta-Flo®)

PREPARATION

- Gather all the ingredients and supplies. Put them on a tray.

ACTIVITY

Put the tray on the art table. Have the children put on smocks and push up their sleeves.

Make the PUTTY with the children.

1. Let the children pour one cup of glue and one cup of starch into a large bowl.

2. Let the children take turns stirring with a heavy-duty spoon. Help them. *(This takes a while, so you'll need time and patience.)* Watch the two ingredients blend together.

3. If the PUTTY is too sticky add a little more starch. If it is too thin add a little more glue.

After making the PUTTY, put several trays on the table. Put a small mound of it on each tray and let the children pound, stretch, and poke it.

At the end of the day, put the PUTTY in a covered bowl. Store it in the refrigerator. When you bring it out the next day it will be very cold. *Talk with the children about how it feels.*

COOKED DOUGH

YOU'LL NEED

- 5 cups flour
- 1 cup salt
- 4T alum (spice shelf)
- 2T vegetable oil
- 3 cups water
- Food coloring (optional)

PREPARATION

- Make the DOUGH before school:

1. Boil the water. *(Add food coloring to the water if you want a colored dough.)*

2. Mix all the dry ingredients in a large bowl.

3. Add the boiling water. Stir together.

4. When the mixture is cool enough, put it on a table and knead it until it is thoroughly mixed.

ACTIVITY

Put the dough on the art table. Have the children put on smocks and push up their sleeves.

Let the children push, pound, poke, squeeze, and mold the dough. Encourage them to feel it as they play.

At the end of the day store it in a tightly covered container. Keep it in the refrigerator overnight. If the dough begins to get dry, add a little water.

MORE SOFT DOUGH PLAY

- **Add Textures:** Add sand, confetti, or aquarium gravel to the dough. *Now how does the dough feel? Lumpy? Gritty?*

- **Add Scents:** Add peppermint, vanilla extract, or pumpkin spice. Smells so good!

TEXTURES

PUMPKIN GOOP

YOU'LL NEED

- Corn starch
- Water
- Pumpkin spice
- Large shallow tray
- Measuring cups

PREPARATION

- Gather all the ingredients and supplies. Put them on a tray.

ACTIVITY

Put the tray on a table. Have the children, who are going to help make the PUMPKIN GOOP, put on smocks and push up their shirt sleeves.

Make the GOOP with the children.

1. Pour 1 1/2 cups of corn starch onto the tray.

2. Put a little pumpkin spice on each child's hand and let her add it to the corn starch.

3. Slowly add 1/2 cup of water. Let the children mix the water and scented corn starch together.

After making the GOOP, keep the tray on the table and let the children use their hands to play with it. As they are playing, talk about how it feels and smells.

At the end of the day, put the GOOP in a covered bowl or resealable bag. Store it in the refrigerator.

CLOUD DOUGH

YOU'LL NEED

- Vegetable oil
- Flour
- Water
- Food coloring (optional)
- Large bowl
- Large spoon

PREPARATION

- Gather all the ingredients and supplies. Put them on a tray.

ACTIVITY

Put the tray on the art table. Have the children put on their smocks and push up their sleeves.

Make the DOUGH with the children.

1. Pour 1 cup of water into a small bowl. *(Optional: Add a little food coloring to the water. Let the children watch the food coloring spread through the water. Let them stir it. Now what color is the water?)*

2. Let the children pour 6 cups of flour and 1 cup of oil into a large bowl.

3. Slowly add the water to the flour/oil mixture, letting the children stir as you pour.

4. Continue mixing the ingredients until you get a soft dough. Add a little more water or flour if necessary.

After making the DOUGH, give each child some. Let the children use their hands to play with it for as long as they want. As they are playing talk about how it feels. *Is it slippery? Sticky? Does it smell?*

At the end of the day, put the DOUGH in a covered plastic container or resealable plastic bag. Refrigerate.

TEXTURES

OUTSIDE GOOP
(GREAT ON A WARM DAY!!)

YOU'LL NEED

- Corn starch
- Ice cubes
- Large shallow tray or cake pan
- 1 cup measuring scoop

PREPARATION

ACTIVITY

Bring the ingredients and utensils outside. Have the children wear their smocks.

Make the OUTSIDE GOOP with the children:

1. Pour 2 cups of corn starch onto the tray.

2. Add 12 ice cubes. *(More if you have small cubes.)*

3. Let the cubes melt in the sun.

4. Mix the ingredients until the GOOP is the consistency of white glue.

5. Add more corn starch or several ice cubes if necessary.

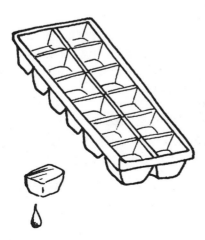

Put the OUTSIDE GOOP under a tree or in a less traveled area of the playground. Let the children enjoy slithering their fingers through it. Keep the GOOP cool and refreshing by periodically adding several more ice cubes and a little cornstarch.

ANOTHER TIME: Freeze colored ice cubes and make COLORED GOOP.

PETROLEUM JELLY FINGER PAINTING

YOU'LL NEED

- Petroleum jelly
- Several large piece of bubble pack
- Tablespoon

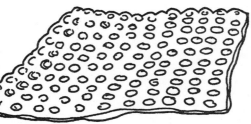

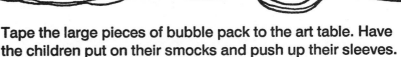

PREPARATION

- None

ACTIVITY

Tape the large pieces of bubble pack to the art table. Have the children put on their smocks and push up their sleeves.

Spoon a small scoop of petroleum jelly on the bubble pack in front of each child as he comes to the art table. Let him smear it on the bubble pack as he chooses. As he's smearing talk about how the bubble pack feels. How the petroleum jelly feels on his hands and fingers. Is it sticky? Slippery?

When he's finished smearing the petroleum around, have him rub his hands together like hand lotion. If he has too much petroleum jelly left on his hands, let him wipe them with a paper towel.

MORE FINGER PAINTING

- Finger Paint and Talk: Sit down and finger paint with the children. This not only makes them feel more comfortable, but makes conversation easier.
- Hand Lotion Finger Painting: Instead of using petroleum jelly, use;
    - Liquid hand lotion on aluminum foil wallpaper.
    - Cold cream on oilcloth.

TEXTURES

FUN WITH SOUNDS

FENCE BAND

YOU'LL NEED

- Metal spoons
- Whisks
- Wooden hammers
- Rubber spatulas
- Plastic rulers
- Medium to wide dowel rods, about one foot long each
- Heavy twine/yarn

PREPARATION

- Set up the FENCE BAND

1. Tie a long piece of twine/yarn on each "musical instrument."

2. Pick a place on your playground fence and tie the "instruments" to it.

ACTIVITY

When the children are outside, let them play in the FENCE BAND. Encourage them to bang, pluck, slide, and tap the fence with the different "instruments." *How do they sound? Which ones make the loudest sounds? Softest?* Play the wooden instruments. *How do they sound?* Play the metal instruments. *How do they sound? Which one is loudest?*

MORE FENCE BAND

- **Sing and Play:** Pick one of the children's favorite songs, such as HAPPY BIRTHDAY. Have the children sing as they play their instruments on the fence.

- **Only Wooden Instruments:** After the children have had many opportunities to play a wide variety of fence instruments, hang only the wooden ones. Let the children play. *Do they all make the same sound?*

ANOTHER TIME: Hang only the metal ones, and let the children play.

SHAKE THE POMPONS

YOU'LL NEED

- Small cheerleader-type pompons
- Marching music

PREPARATION

- None

ACTIVITY

Sit with the children on the floor. Give the children pompons. Have the children hold the pompons up in the air and shake them. *How do they sound?* Shake them slowly. *Can you hear them?* Quickly. *Can you hear them now? Are they louder?* Shake them gently by your ear. *How do they sound?*

Start marching around the room. *Can you hear your feet stomping?* Wave the pompons high in the air as you march. *Do you hear them?*

Turn on the music. Keep marching. Shake the pompons to the beat of the music.

SOUNDS

65

RHYTHM STICK FUN

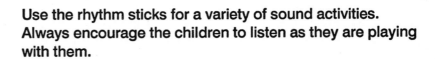

YOU'LL NEED

■ Rhythm sticks

PREPARATION

■ None

ACTIVITY

Use the rhythm sticks for a variety of sound activities. Always encourage the children to listen as they are playing with them.

■ **Tap Sticks On the Floor:** Start tapping your sticks on the floor. Have the children tap with you. When you lift your sticks up in the air, have the children lift theirs. Start tapping again and encourage the children to follow along.

■ **Tap Quietly:** Shh! Tap the floor with your sticks as quietly as you can. Have the children copy you. *How do the sticks sound?*

Continue:

- Tap loudly.
- Tap the floor quietly/loudly with one stick.
- Tap the sticks together quietly/loudly.

■ **Tap To the Rhyme/Song:** Beat/march your sticks on the floor as you say your favorite rhymes and sing your favorite songs. Another time try beating the sticks on the floor while humming the songs you know best.

Try:

- *Johnny Works With One Hammer*
- *Marching We Will Go*
- *Hup 2, 3, 4*
- *Gitty-Up*
- *Happy Birthday*

66

SING FAVORITE SONGS

YOU'LL NEED

- Toilet paper rolls/short dowel rods
- Styrofoam balls

PREPARATION

- Make microphones for the children. Simply push a styrofoam ball onto each toilet paper roll or dowel rod. Tape the balls on. Put the microphones in a dish tub.

ACTIVITY

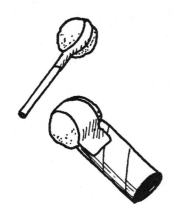

Give all the "singers" a microphone. Let children choose the songs they want to sing. Encourage everyone to sing. *Ask those children who are not singing to listen.* Clap after each song. Here is a list of songs you might want to start with:

Happy Birthday

Wheels On the Bus

Head, Shoulders, Knees, and Toes

Old McDonald

Hokey Pokey

Rock-A-Bye Baby

Ring Around the Rosie

HINT: Take photographs of the "budding" pop singers.

S O U N D S

WAVE YOUR SCARVES

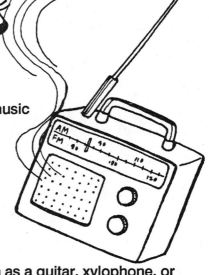

YOU'LL NEED

- Lightweight scarves

- Favorite upbeat music -- Have a variety available

    - Homemade tape of your children's favorite songs/music

    - Popular dance tunes

    - Classical - Waltz of the Sugarplum Fairy, etc.

    - Reggae

    - Marches

    - Instrumental and voice

    - Live music -- an adult who plays an instrument such as a guitar, xylophone, or autoharp

PREPARATION

- None

ACTIVITY

Put on music. Listen to it and begin dancing. As the music is playing, hand each child a scarf. You dance with them, encouraging them to WAVE THEIR SCARVES up high and down low, fast and slow, and in front and behind them. *(Children may take a while to get going, but will soon follow your actions.)*

Play a second piece of music. Listen to it. Let your body move to the new beat. WAVE YOUR SCARVES.

HINTS:

- Have plenty of room for dancing, so the children can spread out and not bump into each other with their scarves or bodies.

- Use your radio, records, tapes, and CD's. Remember, the radio is a very quick resource to a wide variety of popular, classical, and cultural music. Become familiar with the different stations.

68

POTS AND PANS BAND

YOU'LL NEED

■ Variety of unbreakable lightweight pots and pans

■ Wooden spoons

PREPARATION

■ Put the pots, pans, and spoons in a large basket. Set it on an easily accessible shelf.

ACTIVITY

Sit with the children on the floor. Hand each child a pan/pot and a spoon. Begin "playing" the instruments. *How do they sound? Loud? Quiet?*

Children do not need much verbal direction in this activity. They will follow your lead, so when you want to change, just do it and they will copy you.

- Turn your instrument over and continue playing.

- Beat the side of your instrument.

- Switch instruments with a person near you. *How does your new instrument sound?*

- Instead of banging the spoon, slide it back and forth over the pot/pan. *How does this sound? Is it the same as banging?*

- Sit -- Stand -- March in place as you play.

S O U N D S

69

MARCHING HANDS

YOU'LL NEED

■ Nothing

PREPARATION

■ None

ACTIVITY

Sit with the children on the floor. Chant the HUP 2, 3, 4 rhyme. As you're chanting, let your hands keep the beat on the floor. *How do your MARCHING HANDS sound?*

Say the rhyme a little slower/faster, and let your MARCHING HANDS keep the new beat. *How do they sound now?* Shh! Chant with a very quiet voice. *Are your hands marching quietly?* Chant with a very loud voice. *Are your hands marching loudly? Maybe you can't even hear your hands!*

HUP 2, 3, 4

Hup 2, 3, 4 (March hands on floor.)

Hup 2, 3, 4

Hup 2, 3, 4

Let's march on the floor.

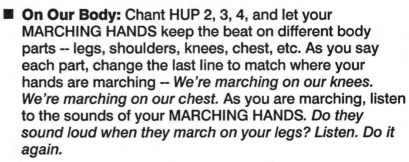

MORE MARCHING HANDS

■ **On Our Body:** Chant HUP 2, 3, 4, and let your MARCHING HANDS keep the beat on different body parts -- legs, shoulders, knees, chest, etc. As you say each part, change the last line to match where your hands are marching -- *We're marching on our knees. We're marching on our chest.* As you are marching, listen to the sounds of your MARCHING HANDS. *Do they sound loud when they march on your legs? Listen. Do it again.*

PLAY YOUR INSTRUMENTS

YOU'LL NEED

- All your instruments *(at least one for every child)*
- Marching music *(optional)*

PREPARATION

- None

ACTIVITY

Sit with the children on the floor. Hand each of them an instrument. Let them play. *How do their instruments sound?*

Play DO AS I DO with the children. You do something with your instrument and the children copy you. You could:

- Play your instrument over your head.
- Play your instrument loudly/softly -- fast/slow.
- Stand up and play your instrument.
- March around the room playing your instrument.
- Sing and play.
- Hum and play.

S O U N D S

71

SHAKE THE EGGS

YOU'LL NEED

■ Lots of large plastic colored eggs

■ Hot glue gun

■ Small objects to put in the eggs, such as:

- Bells
- Buttons
- Pebbles
- Acorns
- Marbles
- Paper clips
- Bobby pins

PREPARATION

■ Make SHAKER EGGS

1. Put several pieces of an object in an egg. Close it. Shake it to be sure it is making the sound you want. Add or subtract objects if necessary. *(Repeat for each egg.)*

2. Hot glue all the SHAKER EGGS closed. *(Safety)*

ACTIVITY

Put all the colorful SHAKER EGGS in your water table. Let the children have fun shaking them and listening to the sounds they make. Encourage the children to shake the EGGS close to their ears. *What do their eggs sound like? Can they find 2 eggs that sound the same when they shake them? Do any eggs sound really loud? Do the children think any eggs are empty? How can they tell?*

ANOTHER TIME: Play **Find the Bells.** Say to the children, *"Let's shake the eggs and see if we can hear one that has bells in it."* Everyone shake the eggs. When someone finds one that has bells, let him shake it for everyone. Then pass it around for everyone to shake and listen to.

MORE SHAKER FUN

■ **Noise Makers:** Instead of SHAKER EGGS, fill the water tub with different baby rattles, squeeze toys, or New Years Eve shakers.

72

CLAP AND MARCH

YOU'LL NEED

■ Nothing

PREPARATION

■ None

ACTIVITY

Start marching around the room. Let the children follow you. After several children have joined the parade, start marching with a noisy step, like stomping. *How does your marching sound? How do your feet feel?*

After a while start clapping as you march. Clap over your head, out in front of you, close to your stomachs, etc. Slowly parade in front of a full length mirror, so everyone can look at himself as he passes by. *Can he see himself clapping? What are his legs doing?*

Come back together. March in place as you continue clapping. Towards the end of the parade, march and clap more slowly and quietly until you've stopped. Shh! Quietly sit down.

**S
O
U
N
D
S**

CRUMBLE THE PAPER

YOU'LL NEED

- Old newspaper
- Scratch paper you can't use
- Several small garbage bags

PREPARATION

- None

ACTIVITY

Have a stack of paper on the floor.

Sit on the floor with several children. Tear the paper into smaller pieces. Shh! Everyone be as quiet as possible. *Can the children hear the paper ripping?* Tear another piece. *Can they hear that one?*

After you've ripped each piece, give it to a child. Have her crumble it up with her hands and put it in the garbage bag. *Can she hear the paper squishing in her hands?* Keep tearing and crumbling until the garbage bag is full. Fill more if you'd like.

PLAY WITH BAGS OF CRUMBLED PAPER

- **Baa, Baa Black Sheep:** Have the bag/s of crumbled paper. Tie it closed. Pass it around as you slowly sing BAA, BAA BLACK SHEEP with the children.

- **Toss and Chase:** Tie the bag/s closed. Take them outside. Let the children toss the bags to each other. Some may want to toss them in the air and catch them.

POP THE BEADS

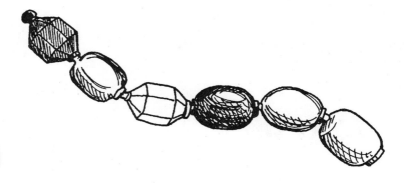

YOU'LL NEED

■ Pop beads

■ Messy tray

PREPARATION

■ None

ACTIVITY

Put lots of colorful pop beads on a messy tray. Set it on a table. Let the children push the beads together and pull them apart. As each child pushes and pulls his beads, encourage him to listen to the noise they make. *Listen. I hear your bead popping. Do you hear it? Pop another bead. Do you hear it now?*

ANOTHER TIME: Play **Pop Goes the Pop Beads!** After the children know how to play with the beads, call out, *"Pop Goes the Pop Beads!"* whenever a child pulls his beads apart. Soon all the children will be saying it as they pop their own beads.

POP! goes the pop beads...

SOUNDS

SOUND LIKE ANIMALS

YOU'LL NEED

■ Nothing

PREPARATION

■ None

ACTIVITY

Sit with the children on the floor. Begin saying the I'M A LION rhyme with them. After you have all pretended to be 4 or 5 different animals, let the children name their favorite animals, and everyone pretend to be it.

ANOTHER TIME: Play **Whisper Sounds.** Let the animals make "whisper sounds." Change the rhyme slightly. For example, *"I'm a lion. Hear me whisper."* The children make quiet "roars."

I'M A LION

Adult: I'm a lion. Hear me.....
Children: Make lion sounds.

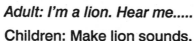

Adult: I'm a bear. Hear me.....
Children: Make bear sounds.

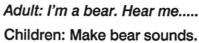

Adult: I'm a snake. Hear me.....
Children: Make snake sounds.

Adult: I'm a monkey. Hear me.....
Children: Make monkey sounds.

CLICK-CLACK

YOU'LL NEED

- Unbreakable measuring cups
- Coffee scoops
- Toilet paper rolls
- Small blocks
- Tiny unbreakable flower pots

PREPARATION

- None

ACTIVITY

Put all the CLICKERS on a messy tray, and set the tray on a table. Encourage the children to pick 2 CLICKERS and clack them together. Listen to the noise. *Can the children make their CLICKERS sound louder? Softer? Try other CLICKERS. Make them sound real loud. Real soft. Does the loud noise hurt anyone's ears?*

SOUNDS

STRUM THE RACKS

YOU'LL NEED

- Wooden, plastic, and rubber mixing spoons
- Heavy-duty tape
- Different slatted metal/wooden racks, such as:
    - Oven rack
    - Grill rack
    - Cooling rack

PREPARATION

- Tape the edges of the rack/s to a table.

ACTIVITY

Put the different types of spoons on the table near the racks. Show the children how to move them back and forth over the slats. Let the children play. As they are STRUMMING THE RACKS, talk with them about the different sounds they are making. *You are really making a loud/quiet noise with your spoon. Here, use this one and see if you can make a quieter/louder noise. (Hand the child a different spoon.)*

While the children are playing, notice if any child is standing off to the side listening to the strumming noises. Bend down and talk to her about what she is hearing. *Does she like the noises? Why? Why not? Are they too loud?* Hand the child you are talking to a spoon, and encourage her to STRUM THE RACKS.

POP GOES THE WEASEL

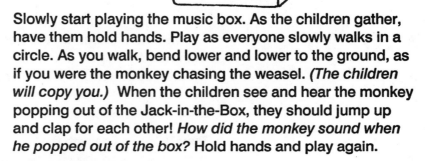

YOU'LL NEED

■ POP GOES THE WEASEL Jack-in-the-Box

PREPARATION

■ None

ACTIVITY

Slowly start playing the music box. As the children gather, have them hold hands. Play as everyone slowly walks in a circle. As you walk, bend lower and lower to the ground, as if you were the monkey chasing the weasel. *(The children will copy you.)* When the children see and hear the monkey popping out of the Jack-in-the-Box, they should jump up and clap for each other! *How did the monkey sound when he popped out of the box?* Hold hands and play again.

ANOTHER TIME: Instead of using the Jack-in-the Box, have all the children sing POP GOES THE WEASEL as they walk around in a circle crouching lower and lower until the last line. Then they pop up.

POP GOES THE WEASEL
All around the cobbler's bench
The monkey chased the weasel.
The monkey thought 'twas all in fun,
POP! Goes the weasel.

S
O
U
N
D
S

79

RING THE BELLS

YOU'LL NEED

■ Wrist bells for all the children

PREPARATION

■ None

ACTIVITY

Sit with the children on the floor. Hand each of them wrist bells. Let them put on the bells and shake their wrists. *How do their bells sound? Who is making their bells sound very quiet? Let's hear. Who is making their bells sound very loud? Let's hear those bells!*

Play DO AS I DO with the children. You shake your bells in a certain way and the children will copy you. You could:

■ Shake the bells over your head. *Can you hear them way up there?*

■ Shake the bells fast. *How do they sound? Gently. Now how do they sound? Stop. Can you hear anything?*

■ Sing songs and shake the bells. *(Start with these 3 songs.)*

■ Hum familiar songs and shake the bells.

ARE YOU SLEEPING
(Ring bells quietly.)

Are you sleeping?
Are you sleeping?
Brother John,
Brother John.

Morning bells are ringing,
Morning bells are ringing.
Ding, ding, dong.
Ding, ding, dong.

LET'S BE FIRE FIGHTERS
(tune: 1 little, 2 little, 3 little children)

Hurry, hurry drive the fire truck.
Hurry, hurry drive the fire truck.
Hurry, hurry drive the fire truck.
On a Sunday morning.

Hurry, hurry turn the corner...

Hurry, hurry find the fire...

Hurry, hurry climb the ladder...

Hurry, hurry spray the water...

Hurry, hurry back to the station.

by Cheryl Luppino and Mary Schuring

HOKEY POKEY - *slightly adapted*
(Children slip bells on their wrists and/or ankles.)

You put your one arm in.
You put your one arm out.
You put your one arm in.
And you shake it all about.

You do the hokey pokey,
And you turn yourself around.
That's what it's all about.

Continue with other body parts:
> *Other arm...*
> *One leg...other leg...*
> *One elbow...other elbow...*
> *Etc.*
> *End with whole self.*

S O U N D S

CLASSROOM SOUNDS

YOU'LL NEED

- Tape recorder
- Blank tape

PREPARATION

- Several days before this activity, be extra aware of all the sounds in your classroom *(bells and buzzers ringing, water running, rattles shaking, rhythm sticks beating, doors closing, toilets flushing, etc.).* Loosely plan a CLASSROOM SOUND WALK.

ACTIVITY

Have your tape recorder in hand. Start walking around the room. Let the children follow you. When you get to the first sound, everybody try to be really quiet. Hold the tape recorder close to the sound and record. Look around for the next sound. Walk to it with the children. Shh! Record. Continue until you have recorded all the sounds you and the children have heard.

Sit down with the children. Play the first sound on the tape. Let the children listen and call out what it is. Continue with all the sounds. Save the tape. Play it often and encourage children to listen. Add more sounds as they naturally occur.

MORE CLASSROOM SOUNDS

- **Favorite Sounds:** Let each child pick a sound. Go over to that sound. Have the child say his name into the recorder and then have him make the sound *(flush the toilet, ring the bell, knock over the stack of blocks, etc.)* and you record it. Continue with other children. Keep the tape and play it often.

82

CHILDREN'S VOICES

Old McDonald had a farm, ee i ee i oo...

YOU'LL NEED
- Tape recorder
- Blank tape

PREPARATION
- None

ACTIVITY

Have the tape recorder in your hand. Walk up to a child and ask her if she'd like to sing a song, make a noise, or say something into the tape recorder. If she wants to, hold the recorder near her mouth. Have her say her name and then sing, talk, or make a special noise. Walk to other children and let them talk, sing, cry, sound like an animal, whisper, etc. into the recorder.

After you've made the tape, sit with the children and play it. Listen carefully to each child's sound. *Who is it?* Repeat what the child said, sang, etc. if you want to. Save the tape and play it often. *(Great activity while you are waiting for lunch or the bus to arrive.)*

MORE CHILDREN'S NOISES

- **Babies Crying:** Have the teacher caring for the babies take the tape recorder for a day. Each time a baby cries, have the teacher say the child's name and then record him crying. Play the BABIES CRYING tape for your children. Listen carefully. *Do all the babies sound the same? What do your children think the babies want when they are crying? Do your children know any of the babies?* Ask the children if they ever cry. *What do they sound like when they cry?*

- **"Big Kids" Noises:** Take a walk around the center, and record sounds that you hear in the older children's rooms, outside, and in the school's offices.

SOUNDS

NEIGHBORHOOD SOUNDS

YOU'LL NEED

- Tape recorder
- Blank tape

PREPARATION

- Several days before this activity, be extra aware of all the sounds in your neighborhood *(construction booming, factories bustling, ducks quacking, cars running, horns honking, water running in streams, birds chirping, sirens blowing, etc.).* Loosely plan a NEIGHBORHOOD SOUND WALK.

ACTIVITY

Have the tape recorder in your hand. Start walking with the children. Tell them to use their ears and listen for sounds. When you or a child hear something, stop. Put the recorder near the sound and record it. Continue walking, listening for and then recording your neighborhood sounds.

When you get back to the classroom, sit on the floor and play the tape. As it plays, have the children call out what they think is making each sound. Stop the tape. Let the children imitate the sound they just heard. *(Save the tape and play it often.)*

CAR NOISES

YOU'LL NEED

- Tape recorder
- Blank tape
- Automobile

BEEEP!

PREPARATION

- Take your tape recorder and a blank tape to your car. Look around and find all the parts that make a specific sound *(door slamming, horn honking, radio playing, wipers whooshing, flashers blinking, seat buckle clicking, motor roaring, etc.)*. Make and record each of these sounds for an appropriate amount of time.

ACTIVITY

Bring the CAR NOISE Tape to group time. Tell the children that you recorded lots of different noises from your car. You want them to listen to the tape, and see if they can tell what part of your car made each noise.

Play the first noise on the tape. Stop the tape recorder. *What was the first noise my car made? (Play over if necessary.)* Turn the recorder on and listen to the next noise. Have the children listen and call it out. Continue listening and trying to recognize each car noise.

Let the children pretend they are driving a car. Encourage them to make different car noises -- beeping horns and roaring motors -- as they drive along.

MORE "NOISY" TAPES

- **Commercial Tapes:** Many music companies have recorded sounds from different vehicles, machinery, etc. Get several and play them for the children. *(Check your local teacher's store/early childhood catalog.)*

- **More Homemade Tapes:** Pick categories you think your children would recognize, and make tapes of the sounds. Try animal sounds, adult voices they would recognize, household tools and appliances such as drills, saws, hammers, vacuum cleaners, mixers, etc.

SOUNDS

FAVORITE STORIES

YOU'LL NEED

- Tote bag
- Tape recorder
- Blank tape for each family

PREPARATION

- Send a note home to your families explaining the FAVORITE STORIES PROGRAM you are starting in your room. Tell the families that:

    1. Each family will receive a calendar to schedule an evening to receive the FAVORITE STORIES Tote Bag with a tape recorder and blank tape in it.

    2. The evening they have the Tote Bag, they should:

        - Have their child pick out his favorite book.

        - Read it to him, recording as they read.

        - Write the name of the book and their child's name on the tape.

    3. Put the tape recorder and story tape in the Tote Bag, and send it back to school the next day with their child.

- Make a calendar, and let all your families have the opportunity to schedule a time to read and record their child's favorite at-home book.

ACTIVITY

Use the FAVORITE STORY TAPES during the day:

(Hearing moms' and dads' voices during the day is soothing and reassuring.)

- **Naptime --** After the children are lying on their cots, play a FAVORITE STORY TAPE. Let the children listen as they fall asleep.

- **Sad --** When a child is feeling lonesome or experiencing some separation anxiety, sit with him and play the FAVORITE STORY TAPE that his mom/dad recorded.

- **Group Time --** Have the actual book that a parent recorded. Instead of you reading it, turn the pages as the parent reads.

SOUNDS AROUND YOUR HOUSE

YOU'LL NEED

- Tape recorder
- Blank tape

PREPARATION

- Have your tape recorder and a blank tape in your house. Look around and find all the places/things that make a specific sound *(door slamming, washing machine slushing, door bell ringing, television playing, vacuum cleaner roaring, dog barking, toilet flushing, people talking, etc.).* Make and record each of those sounds for an appropriate amount of time.

Sit with the children on the floor. Start playing the SOUNDS AROUND YOUR HOUSE Tape. Let the children listen. *Do they recognize any of the sounds? Call them out.* After you've played the whole tape, tell the children that those were sounds from your house.

Play the first sound again. Stop the tape. *What was it? (For example the door slamming.) Do the children have a door in their house? Do they ever slam their door? How does it sound?* Maybe they would like to imitate the sound. Play the next sound, maybe your dog barking. Have the children call out what it is. Tell them a little about your dog. Talk about when he barks, such as when he wants to play or eat. Talk about animals the children have. *While you're talking, have the children make the different animal sounds.*

Before the children go home, tell them to listen for sounds in their houses - toilet flushing, the doors closing, cats meowing, and so on.

S O U N D S

SMALL BOTTLE SHAKE

YOU'LL NEED

- 16 oz plastic soda bottles
- Different dry ingredients to make a variety of sounds, such as:
  - Quiet: cotton balls, paper dots, pompons, cut-up soft tissues, etc.
  - Loud: macrame beads, marbles, colored popcorn kernels, dried corn, etc.
  - Other Interesting Sounds: craft grass, sawdust, colored salt, sand, rice, glitter, etc.
- Hot glue gun

PREPARATION

- Make SMALL SHAKE BOTTLES.

1. Clean and dry all the bottles.

2. Put the ingredient you want in each bottle. Screw on the top and give it several shakes. Do you like the sound? If not, adjust the amount of the ingredient.

3. When you are satisfied with the sound, "hot glue" the top of the bottle to the bottle.
   (Safety: This will make it almost impossible for children to unscrew the bottles.)

ACTIVITY

Put all SMALL SHAKE BOTTLES in a dish tub. Set it on a high shelf so that you can bring it down anytime. Let the children use the bottles at different times. When they do, talk with them about the sounds. Have them shake the bottles slowly, fast, very fast. *Which sound do they like best?*

- **While Waiting:** When children have gathered for an activity, such as lunch, and you are not ready to begin, give each child a SHAKE BOTTLE. Let him shake it. Talk about the different sounds the bottles are making. Switch bottles and shake some more.

- **Outside:** Take the tub outside and set it under a tree. When a child wants to cool off, he can get a BOTTLE and shake.

- **Gathering for Group Time:** As the children come to the group time area, hand each one a SHAKE BOTTLE. They can shake them for as long as they want and then switch with friends.

- **On a Ledge:** Put several BOTTLES on a low shelf or ledge. Let the children shake them as often as they want during free choice. Change them every couple of days.

- **After Dressing To Go Home:** Have the tub of SHAKE BOTTLES near the cubbies. When a child is ready to go home, give her a BOTTLE. Let her shake and listen while the others are still putting on their coats, hats, and boots.

S O U N D S

MORE SHAKE BOTTLES

- **Hold the Handles:** Instead of putting the different ingredients in the 16 oz soda bottles, use clear plastic bottles with handles. *(Dry pet food bottles work well.)* Put the ingredients in them. Let the children hold the bottles by the handles and give lots of shakes. *How do they sound?*

FUN WITH SIGHT

WATCH THE FISH

YOU'LL NEED

- Large aquarium, not less than 15 gallons
- Aquarium gravel
- Seaweed
- Several rocks
- Pump
- Several fish -- large gold fish are hardy and fun to watch
- Fish food
- Small fish net

PREPARATION

- Set up the aquarium the day before you get the fish so that it is ready.

- Put the aquarium on a shelf which is at the children's eye level, but outside their reach. *(Safety: You want the children to easily watch the action in the tank, but not be able to reach up and grab the top of the tank.)*

ACTIVITY

Bring the fish into the classroom. At the beginning of the day, gently put them into the classroom aquarium. Quietly stand near the aquarium and watch them with the children. *What do the fish do? Where do they go?*

After the children get used to the fish in the room, put two or three chairs in front of the aquarium. Sit with the children as they watch the fish. Talk softly about what they see. *(Very soothing and quieting.)*

TUBE POKE

YOU'LL NEED

- Sturdy medium-size box
- Lots of paper towel and toilet paper rolls

PREPARATION

- Make the TUBE POKE BOX

  1. Tape the bottom of the box closed. Cut off the top of the box.
  2. Carefully cut 4-5 holes, the diameter of your tubes, in each side of the box.
  3. Put all the rolls in a dish tub.

S
I
G
H
T

ACTIVITY

Set the TUBE POKE BOX and dish tub on the floor. Let the children look for the empty holes and poke the tubes into them. Some children may want to poke the tubes all the way through so they fall into the box, while others may want to poke the tubes so they just slide partially into the holes. After all the tubes have been poked into the holes, take them out and play again.

MORE TUBE POKE

Individual Tube Poke: Get several heavy duty shoe boxes with tops. Carefully cut 7-10 holes in each top. Put the tops on the boxes. Store paper tubes in each box. When a child wants to play, have her dump out the tubes, put the lid back on the box, and poke the tubes into the holes and pull them out again. Play for as long as each child would like.

LOTS OF MIRRORS

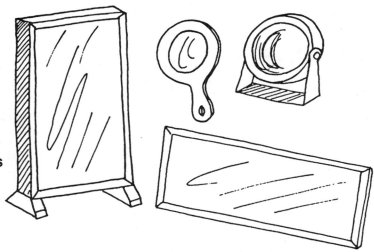

YOU'LL NEED

- Several unbreakable standing floor mirrors
- Unbreakable wall mirror
- Several unbreakable hand mirrors

PREPARATION

- Hang the wall mirror horizontally on an empty wall near the floor.
- Set the hand mirrors in the housekeeping area.
- Stand the floor mirrors in different learning areas.
- Lay one floor mirror horizontally on a long table. Tape it down if necessary.

ACTIVITIES

Watch Me Crawl: Encourage the children to crawl on the floor in front of the wall mirror. They can watch themselves and each other. Talk to the children as they are crawling. Crawl fast - slow. Take "giant" crawls. Crawl like their baby brothers and sisters. Maybe you'll want to crawl with them.

Making Faces: Sit with a child on the floor in front of the wall mirror. Make a happy face. Let the child copy you. Make a sad face. Child copies. Silly face. Child copies. Continue. Maybe two children would like to copy each other. Maybe several children would like to sit and play.

I'm Watching Myself: Encourage the children to watch themselves play. They can easily drive their vehicles, make faces, talk to themselves, build towers, model their dress-up clothes, etc. in front of the closest mirror.

Hat Shop: Put a variety of hats on the table which has the horizontal floor mirror on it. Sit with the children and try on different hats. Look in the mirror. *Which ones do they like?*

Jewelry Shop: Have a basket of old jewelry. Set it on the table with the horizontal mirror. Have several hand held mirrors. Let the children put on and take off the jewelry.

Finger Paint On the Mirror: Lay the floor mirror flat on the art table. *(Tape it to the table if necessary.)* Spray shaving cream on it. Have the children put on paint smocks, and then finger paint on the mirror for as long as each would like. As they finger paint, encourage them to watch their hands move.

**S
I
G
H
T**

TOUCH YOUR EYES

YOU'LL NEED

■ Nothing

PREPARATION

■ None

ACTIVITY

Gather one or more children. Look at them and say, *"Touch your eyes."* Everyone touches his eyes. Clap *hooray* for your eyes. Continue to play by touching and clapping for other facial parts -- nose, cheek, lips, tongue, teeth, chin, forehead, etc.

MORE TOUCH YOUR EYES

Teddy Bear Touch: Hold a teddy bear. Say to a child, *"Touch the teddy bear's eyes."* The child does. Continue to play by asking other children to touch different features on the teddy bear.

In the Mirror: When you and a child are standing in front of a mirror, say to the child, *"Touch your eyes."* Continue to play by giving the child more commands.

COPY ME

YOU'LL NEED

■ Nothing

PREPARATION

■ None

ACTIVITY

Say to the children, *"Watch what I do. Watch what I do."* After saying the chant, do a large or small movement. Then point to the children and say, *"Now you do it. Now you do it."* The children copy the movement they saw you do. After they have done it, clap for them and say *"Stop."* Repeat the activity over and over, always beginning with the chant, *"Watch what I do. Watch what I do."*

**S
I
G
H
T**

Small Movements

Wiggle your nose

Blink your eyes

Open and shut your fingers

Bend your foot up and down

Rotate your head round and round

Scratch like a monkey

Open and close your mouth

Large Movements

Jump up and down

Run in place

Tiptoe in a circle

Fly around in a small area

Crawl

Walk like a duck

Bend up and down

FLOOR PUZZLES

YOU'LL NEED

- Large, simple posters your children will easily identify
- One piece of poster board for each poster
- Spray or watered-down white glue
- Colored markers
- Large resealable plastic bags

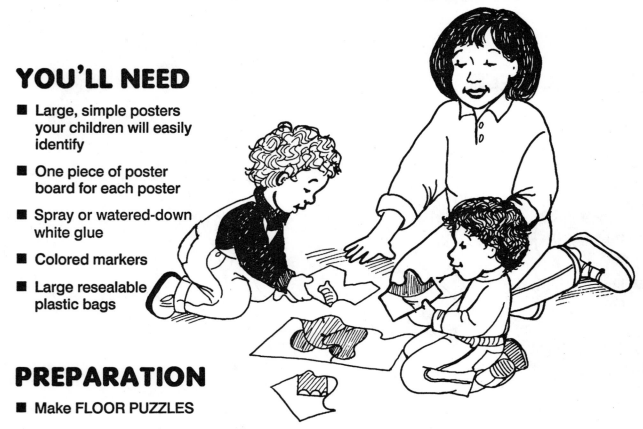

PREPARATION

- Make FLOOR PUZZLES

    1. Glue each poster to a piece of poster board. Let it completely dry.
    2. Cut each poster into 3-5 big pieces or as many as you think your children can put together.
    3. Turn each puzzle over. Make a big dot of the same color on the backs of the pieces of each puzzle. *(Makes sorting puzzle pieces easier.)*
    4. Laminate or cover each piece with clear adhesive paper. Put the pieces of each puzzle in a large resealable plastic bag.
    5. Put all the puzzles in a big tub, so they are handy and easy to bring out.

ACTIVITY

Sit with the children on the floor. Spread out the puzzle pieces, facing right side up. Have the children look at the pieces and help you put it together. As you're doing it, guess what the picture could be. When it is complete, talk about what it really is.

After you've finished, mix up the pieces and put it together again or try a different puzzle.

DRIVE THE CARS

YOU'LL NEED

- 6-8 different small vehicles
- Wide colored tape
- Balance beam or long blocks

PREPARATION

- Put the vehicles in a small bucket or margarine tub

- Make a road in one of several ways. *(Do it differently each time you set up the activity.)*

  1. Put a long piece of colored tape straight along the edge of a large table.
  2. Put a long piece of colored tape on the floor. This time make the tape turn several corners.
  3. Use electrical tape to tape long blocks together in a straight road.
  4. Set the balance beam in a quiet area of the room.

S
I
G
H
T

ACTIVITY

Set up the road in one of the suggested ways. Put the tub of vehicles near the road. Encourage the children to choose vehicles and drive them along the road.

HINT: After the children have done this activity several times, add bridges and tunnels to the roads. You may even want several miniature people.

PEEK-A-BOO

YOU'LL NEED

- Checkers
- Lightweight blanket
- Full-length mirror
- Scarf
- Purse with a zipper

PREPARATION

- None

ACTIVITY

I See You: Walk up to a child. Cover your face with your hands. Slowly move them away, keeping your eyes covered until the end. When your eyes are almost visible, say to the child, *"Peek-a-boo! I see you!"* as you completely remove your hands.

Look For the Checkers: Hide checkers in the sand table. Have the children look for them and put them in a bucket. As a child finds a checker say, *"Peek-a-boo! You see a _____."* Let the child chime in *"checker."*

I See Me: Drape a small blanket over the full length mirror. Tape it to the top. Encourage the children to slowly lift the blanket and look at themselves. *"Peek!"* Clap for those you see playing peek-a-boo with themselves. Ask them, *"Who do you see?"*

Who's Hiding? Have a scarf. Hold it over your face. Say to a child, *"Who do you think is hiding behind this scarf?"* Let the child guess, and then show your face. Give the scarf to the child and let her hold it over her face. You guess who is hiding behind the scarf.

Mystery Purse: Have a mystery purse or drawstring bag. Put something that the children will easily identify inside. Hang it over your shoulder.

When a child asks what's inside, tell him that you'll open it slowly so he can look inside. When he looks, he should try to see what it is. *(Open the zipper or drawstring slowly and then close it quickly.)* Talk about what the child thinks he saw. Do it again and again for that child and others. After a reasonable amount of time, open the mystery purse and take out the object for all to see.

I See You: Walk around the room. When you see a child hiding under a table, behind a cabinet, in a box, etc. bend down and whisper to her, *"Peek-a-boo. I see you!"*

S
I
G
H
T

MATCH THE MITTENS

YOU'LL NEED

■ 4-5 pairs of mittens

■ Messy tray

PREPARATION

■ None

ACTIVITY

Put pairs of mittens on the messy tray and set it on a table. Mix up the mittens. Sit with the children. Have them look at the mittens and find the ones that match. When a child finds a pair, have her put the mittens on. Encourage her to hold up her mittened hands for others to look at. Everyone claps.

Another Time: Put different pairs of socks on the messy tray. When children find mates, talk about who would wear the socks -- Dads? Moms? Babies?

STUFF AND DUMP

YOU'LL NEED

- Several clear plastic bottles

- Lots of things to fit in the bottle *(not dangerously small)*

- Things which are too big to fit in the bottle

PREPARATION

- Cut the tops off each bottle so the openings are slightly larger. Cover the cut edges with pieces of heavy tape.

- Put all the "things" in a big bucket or tub.

ACTIVITY

Put a bottle/s and the bucket of "things" on the table. Let a child stuff his bottle with "things" that fit. *Is anything "too big?" What?* Leave them in the bucket. As he is stuffing, have him look at each one, and you or he call out what each is. Periodically stop and look at all the "things" in the bottle. Point to some of them. Let the child name what you are pointing at. When he wants, let him dump out all of his "things" and stuff the bottle again.

S I G H T

PICK DANDELIONS

YOU'LL NEED

- Area with lots of dandelions
- Unbreakable cup for each child
- Wide dark marker

PREPARATION

- None

ACTIVITY

Let the children pick bouquets of dandelions. As they are picking them, talk with the children about how the dandelions look. *Did anyone find a big dandelion? Small one? Any ants crawling on the dandelions?* After each child has picked as many dandelions as she wants, hold a cup and help her put them in it. Use a marker and write each child's name on her cup. Put the bouquets in a safe place.

Let the children carry the bouquets back to the classroom when it is time to go inside. Put a little water in each one. Set them on a window ledge. During the day encourage the children to look at their bouquets some more, smell them, and touch the flowers and stems. If possible, let the children take their bouquets home.

HAMMER GOLF TEES

YOU'LL NEED

- Large piece of styrofoam such as from packing around a television, computer, or other piece of equipment

- Lots of golf tees

- Several wooden hammers

- Several pairs of safety goggles

PREPARATION

- None

S I G H T

ACTIVITY

Place the piece of styrofoam, golf tees, and hammers on a messy tray. Put the tray on a table. Let the children put on the safety goggles, and hammer as many golf tees into the styrofoam as they want. As they are hammering, remind them to keep their eyes on the golf tees, so they hit the heads of the tees each time they try.

After all the tees have been hammered into the styrofoam, have the children help you pull them out, so they can hammer them back in. You might say, *"Let's look for all the red tees, and pull them out."* Do it. *"Now let's find the green tees, and pull them out."* Continue until all the tees are out. Play again and again.

BIRD WATCHING

YOU'LL NEED

■ Just a nice day

PREPARATION

■ None

ACTIVITY

On a nice day take your children for a walk around the neighborhood. Have as many adults along as possible. As you're walking, look for birds. Watch what they are doing.

■ Sitting on the ground

■ Flying in the sky

■ Searching for food

■ Resting in trees

■ Perched on wires

■ Drinking from puddles

MORE ANIMAL WATCHING

Hang Bird Feeders: Get at least one bird feeder. Hang it so the children can see it from a classroom window. Watch it daily. *What birds go to the feeder? Talk to the birds. (Remember to fill it with bird seed.)*

Inside Animals: Have a rabbit, guinea pig, fish, or other classroom pet. Remember to check your state and local regulations.

More Neighborhood Walks: Instead of looking for birds as you walk, encourage the children to look for worms, caterpillars, and/or ants.

S
I
G
H
T

CAPTURE THE CHIPS

YOU'LL NEED

- Lots of magnetic bingo chips
- Several magnetic wands

PREPARATION

- None

ACTIVITY

Fill the sand table about a quarter to half full of sand. Put all the bingo chips in the sand and mix them up. Lay the magnetic wands in the sand.

Let the children slowly move their wands over the sand, and see how many bingo chips they can capture. Talk with the children about the chips on their wands. Count them. Talk about the colors. Do the children see any chips in the sand? Encourage them to put their wands near the chips they see and try to capture them too.

Help the children take the chips off their wands and hide them in the sand. Play again and again.

SIT AND SCRIBBLE

YOU'LL NEED

■ Sturdy boxes, each one large enough for a child to comfortably sit in

■ Crayons

PREPARATION

■ Cut the tops off the boxes so children can easily climb in and out of them.

ACTIVITY

Set two or three boxes in a quiet area of the room. Have several different colored crayons in each box. Let a child sit or lie inside a box and color it. Maybe several children would like to color together. One could sit inside the box and the other child outside of it. Leave the boxes out for several days. When each one is completely colored, exchange it for another one.

Use the boxes around the room for:

■ Storing toys

■ Sitting in

■ Pushing around the room

■ Doll beds

■ Playing in.

S
I
G
H
T

109

CRAYON MELT

YOU'LL NEED

- Chubby crayons
- Warming tray
- Aluminum foil
- Mittens

PREPARATION

- Let the children help you peel the paper wrapping off the crayons.

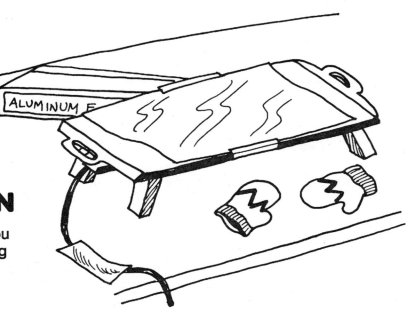

ACTIVITY

Put the warming tray on a table near an electrical outlet. After plugging it in, tape the cord down so no one trips over it. *(Safety)*

When a child wants to color, tape a piece of aluminum foil to the warming tray. As you are taping the foil, have the child put on mittens. Hand the child a crayon or let her choose one.

Encourage her to slowly move the crayon over the foil, watching the crayon melt as she goes. After awhile, ask her if she would like to use a different crayon. If so, switch crayons with her and let her continue to color on the foil. Watch the new color. *What is happening?*

HINT: Offer this activity several days in a row so all the children have an opportunity to do it as often and as long as they want. Children get very involved in this -- it is really fascinating to them to watch what happens to the color.

PLANT THE SEEDS

YOU'LL NEED

- Flower seeds such as zinnias and marigolds
- Potting soil
- Window box
- Rocks
- Small scoops or spoons

PREPARATION

- None

S I G H T

ACTIVITY

Set a messy tray on the table. Put the window box, rocks, dirt, seeds, and scoops on the tray. Let the children help you fill the window box with rocks and dirt. Give each child a seed and let him push it gently into the dirt so that it is covered up. After everyone has had the opportunity to plant a seed, sprinkle the dirt with water.

When you and the children go outside, take the window box. Put it in an untraveled, sunny area. Each day have the children look at the window box. *Do they see any flowers beginning to grow?* Let the children water it when necessary. Continue to watch it. Soon the flowers will begin to grow and after that the colorful blossoms.

PROTECT YOUR EYES

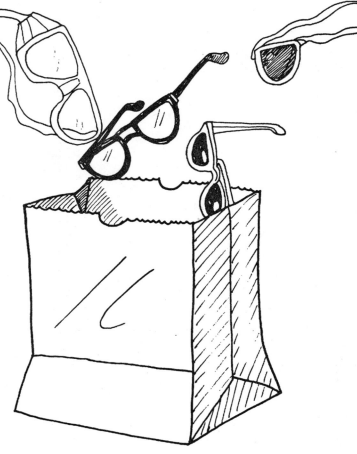

YOU'LL NEED

- Several unbreakable eye glasses
- Several pairs of sun glasses
- Several pairs of safety goggles
- Several eye patches
- Several pairs of swim goggles
- Bag

PREPARATION

- None

ACTIVITIES

Put the eye wear in a bag. Sit with the children on the floor. Put the bag behind your back. Talk with the children about how important their eyes are. Look around the room and have the children each name something they see.

Bring out the bag from behind your back. Tell the children that it is important to protect their eyes.

Eyeglasses: Many people have visual impairments. They wear glasses to help them see clearly. *(Maybe one of the children/adults wears glasses.)* The lenses in the glasses are usually made of safety glass, thus they do not break as easily if the glasses are dropped or damaged. Pass several pairs of eyeglasses to the children and have them try them on. *(Take this opportunity to talk about people who are blind and use special dogs, canes, people, and equipment to help them.)*

Sunglasses: Sometimes the sun is so bright that it hurts your eyes. That is why we have sun glasses. Take out the sun glasses. Put on one pair. Pass the other pairs around and let the children put them on.

Safety Goggles: In the classroom children wear safety goggles when they are hammering. Pull out the safety goggles. Talk about how big they are and how they not only protect the eyes but all the skin and bone around the eyes. Pass them out and let the children try them on.

Eye Patch: Sometimes people hurt their eyes and go to special eye doctors for help. When they treat the eyes, the doctors often tell the patients to cover their eyes with patches while their eyes are getting better. Take out the eye patches and let the children try them on.

Swim Goggles: When people play sports they often wear special goggles to protect their eyes. For example swimmers wear goggles. They are in the water so much that the water irritates their eyes. To protect their eyes, swimmers wear special goggles. Take them out of the bag and pass them around to the children.

EXTENSION

Wear the Eye Gear: Put several different types of eye wear such as the sunglasses and eye patches in the housekeeping area. Let the children wear them as they play. Rotate the different eye wear so the children can use all types. Remember to always have safety goggles available near hammering activities.

S
I
G
H
T

TIP-AND-LOOK BOTTLES

YOU'LL NEED

- Lots of 1 liter soda bottles
- Tornado bottle clamps
- Variety of liquids to put in the bottles:
    - Colored water
    - Mineral oil, water, and food coloring
    - Vegetable oil and water
    - Soapy water
- Variety of small "things" to put in the bottles
    - 1 teddy bear or dinosaur counter
    - 2 or 3 marbles
    - Sequins
    - Glitter
    - Different sizes and colors of buttons
    - Small flat plastic fish

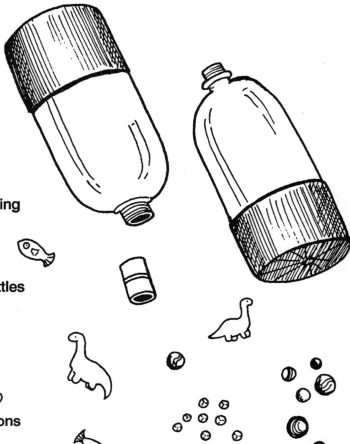

PREPARATION

Make TIP AND LOOK BOTTLES.

1. Decide which liquid and/or "things" you want in the bottles.

2. Pair the plastic bottles. Fill one bottle in each pair. Leave the other one empty.

3. Connect each full and empty pair of bottles by hot gluing the tornado clasp to the tops of the bottles. *(Safety.)*

ACTIVITY

Sink the Bear/Dinosaur: Encourage the children to tip the bottle upside-down and watch the teddy bear/dinosaur sink to the bottom of the other bottle.

Marble Drop: Set up several of these, each with a different liquid. Watch the marbles move slowly - quickly - and all speeds in between.

Soapy Water: Two year olds love to shake things. Let the children shake the bottles with soapy water and watch the bubbles form and disappear. *Are there lots of bubbles in their bottles? Just a few? Make more!*

Floating Buttons: Put different colored buttons in a mixture of mineral oil and water. Move the bottle around. Look at certain buttons. *What colors are they? Do you see big ones?* Watch them float around the water. Lay the bottle horizontally on a shelf at the children's eye level. Watch the buttons slowly move around.

Color Bonanza: Add lots of colored glitter to clear water. Tip the bottle back and forth and watch the glitter dance through the water.

Watch the Sequins: Put a variety of sequins in clear water. Shake the bottle. Tip the bottle. Roll it on the floor. *What is happening to the sequins?*

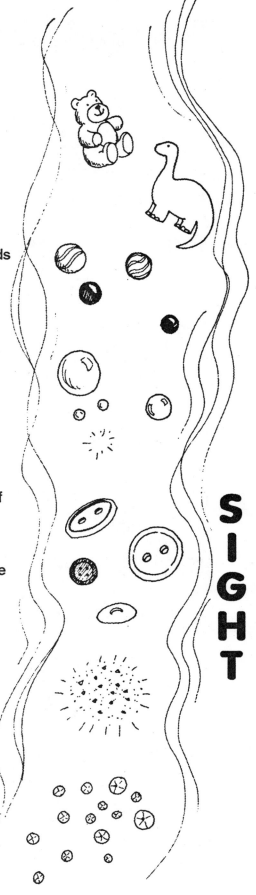

S
I
G
H
T

115

BUBBLE BLOWING FUN

YOU'LL NEED

■ Empty bubble containers with wands -- at least one for each child

■ One or more full bubble container/s and wand

PREPARATION

■ None

ACTIVITY

CATCH THE BUBBLES -- You blow real bubbles from your bottle. The children can:

- Catch the bubbles on their hands and arms.

- Catch the bubbles on their wands and "put them" in their empty bottles.

- Catch the bubbles on pieces of white duplicating paper. Encourage the children to look carefully. *Can they see where their bubbles landed?* Blow more bubbles and let the children catch them again.

POP THE BUBBLES -- Blow bubbles up in the air. Let the children watch them float and when they get within reach, pop them with their hands. *(Clap for the popped bubbles.)*

STOMP THE BUBBLES -- Blow the bubbles in front of you. Watch them carefully. When they are about to land on the floor, let the children "stomp" them with their feet. Blow some more and play again -- and again -- and again.

HINT: If you play this inside have a towel ready to wipe the floor so it does not get too slippery.

LOOK AT THE ANIMALS

YOU'LL NEED

- Messy tray
- Salt
- Large, colorful pictures of animals
- Poster board

PREPARATION

- Prepare the PICTURE BOARDS

  1. Cut poster board to fit in a messy tray.
  2. Glue the animal pictures to the poster board.

ACTIVITY

Set the PICTURE BOARD on the messy tray. Pour salt over the entire piece of poster board, being sure to hide the animals. Put the tray on the table.

Let the children gently move the salt around the tray looking for the animals. When they find one, name it and talk about how he looks. *What sound does he make?* Listen to each other pretend to be the animal. Cover the animal back up, and look for another one.

MORE HUNTING

Different Boards: Make different boards to add variety to the game:

- Different pictures of babies, teddy bears, toys, etc.

- Large different colored construction paper circles.

- Easy seasonal pictures -- children building snow people, etc.

SIGHT

FUN WITH FOODS

GELATIN "COOKIES"

INGREDIENTS

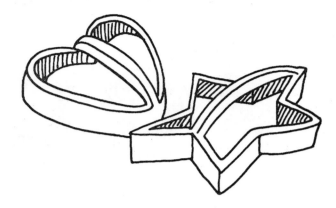

- 3 T *(envelops)* unsweetened gelatin
- One 12oz can frozen juice concentrate
- 2 cups water
- 9"x13" baking dish

BASIC RECIPE

Thaw the juice concentrate and pour it into a large bowl. Add the gelatin to the concentrate. Boil the water. Pour the boiling water into the gelatin mixture, and stir until the gelatin is dissolved.

Lightly grease the dish. Pour the mixture into the dish and set in the refrigerator for several hours until firm. Cut the gelatin into individual squares and set them on a plate. Cover until ready to serve.

Making GELATIN "COOKIES" With Children
(Remember to have the "cooks" wash their hands.)

- Pass the can of frozen juice concentrate to each child. *How does it feel? Shake it. What do you hear?*

- Shake the concentrate into a bowl and set it on a low shelf. Encourage the children to watch it thaw. *What is happening to the juice?*

- Let several children pour the gelatin into the bowl. Walk to each child, set the bowl in front of her, and let her stir the gelatin and thawed concentrate together. Continue until everyone has had an opportunity to stir.

- Remember Safety: Away from the children, add the boiling water, stir, and pour into a dish. Refrigerate.

- After the gelatin has hardened set it on the table. Have several cookie cutters. Help the children each cut a GELATIN "COOKIE." They'll eat it right away. After everyone has eaten his "COOKIE" have fun eating the leftover pieces. *What do they look like?*

EASY PIZZAS

INGREDIENTS

- English muffins
- Pizza sauce
- Shredded cheese
- Optional -- Children's favorite toppings such as:
  - Pepperoni
  - Sliced mushrooms
  - Sliced olives
  - Drained pineapple bits

BASIC RECIPE

Spread pizza sauce on the English muffins. (*Optional: Add the toppings.*) Cover with shredded cheese. Toast the pizzas in the broiler or toaster oven until the cheese has melted. Put them on a plate and cover with aluminum foil until snack.

Making EASY PIZZAS With Children

(Remember to have the "cooks" wash their hands.)

- Have a teaspoon for each "cook." Put a little pizza sauce on each child's muffin. Let the children use the spoons to spread their pizza sauce around the muffin.

- Give children who want it, some pepperoni. Let them put it on their pizzas. *What does the pepperoni smell like?* Let each child add more toppings to his pizza if he chooses to do so.

- Have small bowls of shredded cheese on the table. Let the children take some and sprinkle it on top of their pizzas.

- Have each child set his pizza on the broiler pan.

- Eat them warm. *How do they feel? Look at the cheese. What happened to it? Smell your pizza. Does it smell like the pizza you have at home? How does it taste? Do you like it? Does it feel warm in your mouth?*

FOODS

121

PEANUT BUTTER BALLS

INGREDIENTS

- 18 oz jar of low-fat peanut butter
- 6t honey
- 2-3 cups of non-fat dry milk *(enough to give the mixture a dry consistency)*
- Raisins

BASIC RECIPE

Mix all of the ingredients together in a large bowl. Scoop out small amounts of dough and roll them into balls. Set them on a plate and cover until snack time. Put the raisins in a bowl for children to stick on at snack time.

Instead of having raisins in a bowl, have cereal, oyster crackers, or other small bits of food.

Making PEANUT BUTTER BALLS With Children
(Remember to have the "cooks" wash their hands.)

- Let the children stir the peanut butter and honey together. *Is anyone getting peanut butter on her hands? How does it feel? Can you smell it?*

- Let a child pour one cup of dry milk in the bowl. Set the bowl in front of each child and let him stir. *Is it hard to stir the dry milk and peanut butter?* Hold the spoon with him if he needs help. Add a second cup of dry milk and continue to let the children stir.

- Give each child a scoop of peanut butter. Let him make it into a snake, ball, or whatever he wants. Have raisins *(cereal, oyster crackers, etc.)* in a bowl. Let him stick raisins into his shape. Eat right away. *How do they taste? Can you smell the peanut butter? Can you see any of the dry milk? Where do you think it went? Can you feel the raisins in your mouth? How do they* taste?

CEREAL BALLS

INGREDIENTS

- 3 cups cereal such as shredded wheat or corn flakes
- 2T honey
- 5T peanut butter
- Milk as needed

BASIC RECIPE

Pour the cereal in a blender and mix. Add the honey and peanut butter. Mix again. Slowly add milk and blend until you have a dough-like consistency. Put the mixture in a bowl and cover. Refrigerate. After the mixture is cold, make them into balls and put them on a plate. Refrigerate until snack.

Making CEREAL BALLS With Children
(Remember to have the "cooks" wash their hands.)

- Give each child a little cereal to taste. *Do they ever eat this cereal at home? Do they like it?*

- Let the children pour small amounts of cereal into a blender. *Turn it on and watch the cereal "fly" around -- listen to it crunch. Turn off the blender -- so quiet.*

- After the mixture has cooled in the refrigerator, give the children a little and let them make balls and shapes. *Do the balls feel cold?* Eat right away. *How do they taste?* Have the children chew slowly. *Can they feel the cereal in their mouths?*

F O O D S

PRETZEL "SNAKES"

INGREDIENTS

- 1 pkg yeast
- 1 ½ cups warm water
- 1t salt
- ½t sugar
- 4 cups flour
- 1 beaten egg
- Coarse salt *(optional)*

BASIC RECIPE

Measure the warm water into a large mixing bowl. Sprinkle the yeast over the water and stir until it looks soft. Add the salt, sugar, and flour. Mix and knead the dough. Cover the bowl, set it in a warm place, and let the dough rise until doubled. *(About an hour.)* Punch the dough down and divide it into small pieces. Roll and form into pretzel shapes.

Grease the cookie sheets and lay the pretzels on them. Brush each pretzel with beaten egg and sprinkle with a little coarse salt. Bake at 425 degrees for 12-15 minutes.

Making PRETZEL "SNAKES" With Children
(Remember to have the "cooks" wash their hands.)

- Let the children help you put the salt, sugar, and flour in the bowl.

- Sprinkle flour on the table. Have the children use their palms to slowly spread it all around. *(This will get flour on their hands, as well as on the table.) How does the flour feel? Is it slippery?*

- Put the dough on the floured table and let the children help you knead it. *Does it smell?* Have the children look at their hands. *What do they see? How do they feel? Are they sticky?*

- Let the children help you cover the bowl and set it in the sun. Remind them that they need to tiptoe near the bread. *"Shh! It is resting."* Periodically uncover the bowl, and let the children see what is happening. *Talk about what is happening to the dough.*

- After it has risen, put more flour on the table, and give each child a little dough. Let him make a ball, snake, or whatever from the dough. When finished put them on the cookie sheet and bake. *Can you smell them?*

- Put soft cheese in a bowl, and let the children dip their warm pretzels in it. *How do they taste?*

CIRCLES AND SQUARES

INGREDIENTS

- 2 cups apple juice
- 2 cups water
- 6T (envelops) of plain gelatin
- 6 oz unsweetened red raspberry gelatin
- Two 9"x13" baking dishes

BASIC RECIPE

Pour all the raspberry gelatin and plain gelatin in a large bowl. Pour 1 cup of apple juice and 1 cup of water into a pan and bring it to a boil. Slowly pour it into the gelatin mixture, stirring constantly until the gelatin is thoroughly dissolved. Pour the other cup of apple juice and water into the mixture and stir together.

Lightly grease the two dishes. Pour the mixture into the dishes and set in the refrigerator for several hours until firm. Cut the hardened gelatin into circles and squares and set them on a plate. Cover until ready to serve.

Making CIRCLES AND SQUARES With Children
(Remember to have the "cooks" wash their hands.)

- Let the children help you pour the gelatin into the large bowl. *Can you smell the powder? Do you like how it smells?*

- Remember Safety: Away from the children boil the water and juice, and then add it to the gelatin mixture. Stir it until the gelatin has dissolved and the mixture has cooled down to a safe temperature. Bring it back to the children. Let them help you add the remaining apple juice and water.

- Let each child stir the mixture. *Smell the gelatin as you're stirring.*

- After the gelatin has hardened set it on the table. *How does it look now? Did it change?* Have circle and square cookie cutters. Let each child cut the shape he wants and then eat it. *How does it taste?*

- Talk about how the gelatin "feels" in their mouths. *Does it melt?* Swallow slowly. *Does it feel like water? Taste like water?*

F O O D S

125

THUMB PRINT COOKIES

INGREDIENTS

- 2 cups flour
- 1t salt
- 2/3 cup oil
- 4-5T water
- Low fat peanut butter

BASIC RECIPE

In a large bowl, mix the first four ingredients together using a fork. Roll the dough into small balls. Press a thumb print in each one.

Preheat the oven at 400 degrees. Bake the cookies on a greased cookie sheet for 8-10 minutes. Let the cookies cool. Fill the "thumb prints" with peanut butter.

Making THUMB PRINT COOKIES With Children

(Remember to have the "cooks" wash their hands.)

- Let the children help you pour the ingredients into the bowl.

- Walk to each child, set the bowl in front of her, and let her use a fork to stir the ingredients together.

- After the ingredients have been totally mixed, give each child a little bit and let her make it into a ball and set it on the cookie sheet.

- Put peanut butter in a dish. Have popsicle sticks nearby. Put the waste basket next to the table. After the cookies have baked and cooled, let each child scoop a little peanut butter on a stick and put it on her cookie. *(She will probably want to lick the excess peanut butter off the stick and then throw it away. How did it taste?)* Have the cookies for snack along with a glass of milk/juice. *How do the cookies taste? Can the children still taste the peanut butter?*

126

JUICE POPS

INGREDIENTS

- One of your children's favorite juices such as:
    - Pineapple juice
    - Grape juice
    - Cranberry juice
- Popsicle sticks
- Small paper cups
- Small eatable treats, such as raisins or grapes (optional)

BASIC RECIPE

Fill the paper cups about 3/4 full of juice. Put the cups in the freezer. When the juice begins to freeze, put a popsicle stick in the middle of each cup. When frozen, wiggle the popsicles out of the cups. Give a popsicle and cup to each child. Great for an outside snack on a warm day.

Optional: Let the children put one or two "treats" in their popsicles along with the popsicle sticks.

Making JUICE POPS With Children
(Remember to have the "cooks" wash their hands.)

- Make the juice from concentrate. Let the children pour the concentrate and water into a covered unbreakable container. Pass the container around, and let the children shake it until the juice is completely mixed. *Watch what happens to the juice.*

- Let children hold the cups as you pour the juice into them.

- Let the children add "treats" to the juice.

- Once the JUICE POPS begin to freeze, give each child a popsicle stick to put in a cup.

- Take the frozen JUICE POPS outside and have them in a shady area. *How do they taste? How do they feel inside the children's mouths? Cold? Do the children swallow their bites whole? Do they let the JUICE POPS melt inside their mouths?*

FOODS

JUICY SLUSH

INGREDIENTS

- Orange juice concentrate or any other juice your children like
- Ice cube trays

BASIC RECIPE

Make the orange juice. Pour it into the ice cube trays and freeze. Put the orange juice cubes into the blender and turn it on and off until the cubes reach a slushy consistency. Spoon the slush into paper cups. Have for snack.

Making JUICY SLUSH With Children
(Remember to have the "cooks" wash their hands.)

- Let the children pour the juice concentrate and water into a covered unbreakable container. Pass the container around, and let the children shake it until the juice is completely mixed. *How does the juice look now?*

- Put the empty ice cube trays on the table. Have the children hold them as you pour juice into each section. *Is it hard to hold them still? Thank you for trying so hard.*

- After the juice is frozen, crack the cubes. Hand one to each child and have her put it in a blender. *How do the juice cubes feel?*

- Encourage the children to watch and listen to the blender as you quickly turn it on and off. *What is happening? How does the blender sound?*

- Have the drink right away. *How does it taste? Is it cold in their mouths?*

PUDDING POPS

INGREDIENTS

- Unsweetened instant pudding
- Additional ingredients specified by the recipe
- Large bowl
- Mixing spoon
- Ice cube tray
- Popsicle sticks

BASIC RECIPE

Follow the directions on the package and mix the pudding. Spoon pudding into each section in the ice cube tray - enough for everyone. Put the ice cube trays in the freezer. When the PUDDING POPS are partially frozen, put a popsicle stick in each one. Let the POPS completely freeze. Pop them out of the ice cube trays and serve for snack.

Making PUDDING POPS With Children
(Remember to have the "cooks" wash their hands.)

- Put the large bowl on the table. Let the children pour the pudding mix into it. *Smell it as you pour.*

- Have the other ingredients nearby. Name each one, and then have the children help you put them in the bowl. *How do they look in the bowl?*

- Put the bowl in front of each "cook" and let him stir the ingredients together. *Watch what happens to the ingredients. Now how does the pudding smell?*

- Hand each child a spoon and let him put some pudding into a section of the ice cube tray.

- Give each child a popsicle stick to put in each section.

- Before you put the ice cube trays in the freezer have each child feel the tray. *Is it cold? Warm?* Tell the children that you are going to put it in the freezer. When you take it out, you want them to touch it again and see if it is still warm. *(Remember to do it.)*

- Enjoy the popsicles for snack. *Do they still smell like pudding? How do they taste?*

F O O D S

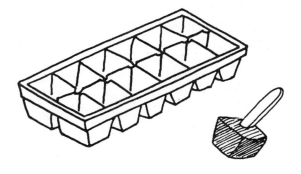

129

FRESH FRUIT SHAKE

INGREDIENTS

- 1 quart of orange or pineapple juice from concentrate or any other juice your children like
- 2 frozen bananas
- 2 cups frozen unsweetened strawberries or any other fruit your children like

BASIC RECIPE

Make the juice. Pour the juice, bananas, and strawberries in a blender. Turn on and off until the SHAKE is smooth. Pour in small paper cups and have for a cooling snack.

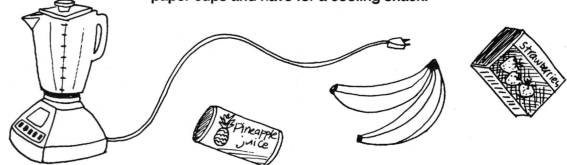

Making FRESH FRUIT SNACK With Children
(Remember to have the "cooks" wash their hands.)

- Let the children pour the juice concentrate and water into a covered unbreakable container. Pass the container around and let the children shake it until the juice is totally blended. Take the cover off. Walk to each child and let him smell it. *What do you think?*

- Put the blender on the table. Peel the bananas. Break them into pieces and give them to the children. Let them put the bananas in the blender.

- Next give the children strawberries to put in the blender.

- Slowly pour the juice into the blender. Cover it. Have the children watch and listen to the blender as you turn it on and off. *Where did the bananas go? Where are the strawberries? What color is your drink?* Slowly take the top off the blender. *Ask the children to smell as you do it. What do they smell?*

- Pour the SHAKES into small paper cups and drink right away. Have the children take a sip. *Do they taste the bananas? Strawberries? Do they like their shakes?*

YOGURT SHAKES

INGREDIENTS

- 24 oz plain low-fat yogurt
- 3 bananas
- 1 ½ cups cold apple juice
- 1 ½ cups cold milk
- 3T honey *(optional)*

BASIC RECIPE

Put the yogurt and bananas in a blender. Mix them together until smooth. Pour this mixture into a large pitcher. Add the cold juice, milk, and honey to taste. Stir until combined. Take the pitcher and small glasses outside. Pour the drink and enjoy in the shade.

Making YOGURT SHAKES With Children
(Remember to have the "cooks" wash their hands.)

- Have a tablespoon or small scoop. Let the children spoon the yogurt into the blender. *(You might want to have small plastic teaspoons for the children to use to have a quick taste of the plain yogurt. Throw the spoons away.)*

- Peel the bananas and break them into pieces. Let the children put the bananas in the blender and then watch them while you are running the blender. *What happened to the bananas?*

- Pour all the ingredients in a large pitcher. Pass the pitcher to each "cook" and let him stir the mixture together. *Can they smell bananas? Strawberries? What does the drink smell like?*

- Put the pitcher in the refrigerator until you go outside. Take the drink and small cups with you. Pour a little bit for each child. *How do they like it? Can they taste the yogurt? Bananas?*

**F
O
O
D
S**

131

PICNIC PUNCH

INGREDIENTS

- 6 oz can frozen lemonade concentrate
- 6 oz can frozen limeade concentrate
- 1 cup water
- 1 liter bottle chilled gingerale
- Ice *(optional)*

BASIC RECIPE

Thaw the juice concentrates in a large unbreakable pitcher. Blend them well with a cup of water. Refrigerate until ready to have with the children. Stir the juice just before pouring and then add the gingerale. Pour into small glasses and enjoy with the children.

Making PICNIC PUNCH With Children
(Remember to have the "cooks" wash their hands.)

- Put the frozen concentrates in a clear unbreakable container with a cover and set it on a low shelf. *Watch them thaw. What colors are they?* After thawed, add the water and let the children shake the container until the juice is mixed. *What color is the juice now? Shh! Can they hear the juice mixing?* Slowly take the top off the container. *Smell. Good?*

- Make one of the children's favorite simple snacks with them. Put it in a picnic basket.

- Have the children help you carry the picnic snack, juice, gingerale, and cups outside.

- Sit in a shady area. Pour the gingerale into the juice. Walk to each child and let him take a picnic snack. Eat with the children. After the snack let each child hold his cup while you pour his drink. *Is it cold? Good?*

HOMEMADE BUTTER

INGREDIENTS

- Unbreakable covered jar
- Pint of whipping cream for every 5 children
- Pinch of salt *(optional)*

BASIC RECIPE

Pour the whipping cream into the jar. Tightly cover it and shake until butter forms. Pour off the liquid that forms on top. Add a pinch of salt. Put the butter in a tub. Have the butter with crackers for a snack.

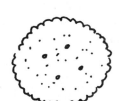

Making HOMEMADE BUTTER With Children
(Remember to have the "cooks" wash their hands.)

You'll Need: Small unbreakable covered jar for each child.

- Let the children pour the whipping cream into the jars.

- Put the jars on a table. Have the children take turns holding a jar and shaking it. You might also want to let the children roll it on the table. After a while the cream with begin to form into butter. Keep shaking/rolling until the butter completely forms. *Watch the whipping cream change into butter as everyone shakes/rolls the jars. Listen the cream in the beginning. How does the butter sound at the end?* Take the top off the cream before it becomes butter. *Let the children smell it.* Do this several times.

- Have small crackers on a plate. Let the children spread a little butter on the crackers, and eat them right away. How does the butter taste? Let the children spread another cracker with butter. This time have them put just a pinch of salt on their butter. Eat this cracker. *How does the butter taste now? Can they taste the salt?*

F
O
O
D
S

PAINTED TOAST

INGREDIENTS

- Bread
- Milk
- Food coloring
- Toaster
- Pastry brush or cotton swabs

BASIC RECIPE

Pour the milk into several small containers. Add a different food coloring to each container. Mix. Brush several pieces of bread with colored milk. Pop them in the toaster and toast. After toasting, cut the colored bread into quarters. Put them on a plate, and have for snack with a glass of juice or milk.

Making PAINTED TOAST With Children
(Remember to have the "cooks" wash their hands.)

You'll Need: Clear unbreakable containers to mix the milk.

- Have the children watch you pour the milk into several clear containers. *What color is the milk?* Squeeze a little food coloring into the first container. Encourage the children to watch the milk. *What is happening?* After a bit, let the children stir the milk with a small spoon. *Now what color is the milk?* Color the other milks in the same manner.

- *(Cut the bread in half. Have the toaster on the table. Tape the electric cord down for safety.)* Let each "cook" brush/swab her own color on her half-slice of bread. As each child is finished, pop her colored bread in the toaster. How does it smell? Listen/watch for the colored toast to pop up. *Hear the pop?* Let each child eat her warm, colored toast right away. *How does the warm toast feel in her hands? Does she like the colors? How does it taste in her mouth? Can she hear the toast crunch as she chews it? Shh. Listen.*

- Look at the table when you are finished. *Lots of toast crumbs?* Let the children help you sponge it off.

134

EASY MUFFINS

INGREDIENTS

- Favorite easy corn muffin mix -- try a different muffin mix each time
- Additional ingredients specified by the recipe
- Cinnamon

BASIC RECIPE

Follow the recipe on the box. After making the muffins, sprinkle a little cinnamon on top. Bake them according to the directions. When finished, put the muffins on a plate and cover until snack. Have them with a glass of milk.

Making EASY MUFFINS With Children
(Remember to have the "cooks" wash their hands.)

- Have all the ingredients nearby. Pour the mix into a large bowl. *Let the children smell it.*

- Add the rest of the ingredients. Have a whisk. Pass the bowl to each child. Stand behind each child and hold the bowl. Let him stir the ingredients. *(Help if necessary.) Watch what happens. Talk about it.*

- Let the children spoon the muffin mix into the muffin pan. Have the cinnamon. Hand the cinnamon to each child, and let him sprinkle some on a muffin. *Smell. Oh so good!*

- Eat the muffins while they are still warm. Encourage the children to eat slowly. *Smell the muffins before they eat. Can they feel the muffins in their mouths? How do they feel? Warm? How do they taste? Delicious? Gritty?*

F O O D S

EASY PUMPKIN PIE

INGREDIENTS

- Canned pumpkin
- Additional ingredients specified by the recipe on the can of pumpkin
- Pre-made pie crust

BASIC RECIPE

Follow the recipe on the can of pumpkin and the package of pie crust. Bake. Put the pumpkin pie on the table at snack time. Have plates. Safely cut the pie into small pieces, and let the children have with a glass of milk.

Making EASY PUMPKIN PIE With Children
(Remember to have the "cooks" wash their hands.)

- Have all the ingredients plus a large bowl and a whisk. Follow the recipe. At each step let the children mix the ingredients with the whisk. Go slowly. *Talk about how the different ingredients smell.*

- Let the children spoon the pie filling into the crust.

- Bake the pie. *If the oven is near remind the children to smell the pie as it is baking.* Periodically look at and smell it.

- At snack time cut the pie with the children. *Talk about how good it looks and smells.* Have it with a glass of milk.

PUMPKIN BREAD

(thank you Kathleen Baxter, COME AND GET IT)

INGREDIENTS

- ½ cup vegetable oil
- ½ cup honey
- 1t molasses
- 2 cups pumpkin
- 2 cups whole wheat flour
- 2t baking soda
- 1t ground cloves
- 1t cinnamon

BASIC RECIPE

Cream the oil and honey. Add the molasses and pumpkin and mix all the moist ingredients together. In another bowl combine all the dry ingredients. Combine the moist and dry ingredients into one bowl and mix them together.

Grease a 5"x9" loaf pan. Pour the batter into the pan. Bake at 350 degrees for about 45 to 60 minutes. Test with a toothpick. Loosen the sides and cool on a wire rack.

Making PUMPKIN BREAD With Children

(Remember to have the "cooks" wash their hands.)

- Hold each moist ingredient so the children can smell it before you pour it into the bowl. Have the children mix the ingredients together with a wooden spoon.

- Let the children smell the flour and spices, and then put them in the bowl.

- Put the bowl in front of each child, and let her stir the ingredients. *Remember to smell the batter as it is being mixed.*

- After the BREAD has cooled, put it on the table and cut it with the children. *Can they smell it as you cut?* Have the children put their hands just above the bread. *Can they feel the heat?*

- Give each child a piece of BREAD. As you're eating, talk about all the things you used to make the BREAD. *Can they smell them? Pumpkin? Cinnamon? How does the BREAD taste?*

FOODS

SMELL THE CINNAMON

INGREDIENTS

- Children's favorite snacks that are even better with cinnamon, such as:

    - Applesauce
    - Toast
    - Apple wedges
    - Plain low-fat yogurt
    - Banana chunks
    - Graham crackers

- Cinnamon in a shaker

BASIC RECIPE

Choose the snack for the children. Prepare it as you normally would, and set it on a plate until snack. Serve the snack. Pass the cinnamon shaker, and let each child shake cinnamon on his snack.

   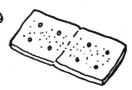

Making SMELL THAT CINNAMON With Children
(Remember to have the "cooks" wash their hands.)

- **Applesauce:** Put the applesauce in a large bowl. Pass the bowl to each child, and let her scoop some onto a small plate. *(Repeat for each child.)* Give the cinnamon shaker to each child, and let her shake some on her applesauce. *How does it smell?*

- **Toast:** Toast bread with the children. When it pops up, cut it in half and put a piece on each child's plate. Hand her the cinnamon shaker. Let her shake some on her toast. *How does it taste?*

- **Apple Wedges:** Cut apple wedges and put them on a plate. Let the children help themselves and then sprinkle cinnamon on them.

- **Yogurt:** Let the children scoop a little yogurt on their plates. Pass the cinnamon shaker, and let the children shake cinnamon on their snacks. *Encourage the children to smell the yogurt as they eat it.*

- **Banana Chunks:** Peel the bananas with the children. Break them into chunks. Give one to each child. Pass the cinnamon shaker, and let each child shake a little cinnamon on his banana. *Have the children hold their bananas to their noses and smell. Good? Eat them with a glass of milk.*

- **Graham Crackers:** Pass the graham crackers to the children. Hand each child the cinnamon shaker, and let her shake a little cinnamon on her cracker. *How does it taste?*

QUICK & TASTY PUDDING

INGREDIENTS

- Children's favorite unsweetened pudding
- Additional ingredients specified by the recipe on the box

BASIC RECIPE

Pour the pudding mixture in a large bowl. Make the pudding according to the directions on the box. Pour it into small bowls. Put on a tray and cover. Keep it in the refrigerator until snack.

Making QUICK AND TASTY PUDDING With Children
(Remember to have the "cooks" wash their hands.)

- Make puddings which the children have probably never tasted. Try banana or pistachio. *Talk about how the pudding smells as you're mixing it. How does it taste? Does the banana pudding taste like real bananas?*

- Let the children pour the pudding mixture and all the ingredients into a large bowl. Give a child a wire whisk. Put the bowl in front of him, and let him stir the ingredients. Pass the bowl to the next child and let her stir. Continue until the children have all stirred the pudding and it is well mixed. *How does it look? Smell?*

- Let the pudding rest for a couple of minutes in the middle of the table. As the children are waiting for the pudding to set up, sing favorite songs with them. Maybe OLD McDONALD HAD A FARM. The children can make all the animal noises as they sing. When they're done, the pudding should be ready.

- Serve the pudding. *Talk about how it tastes.*

FOODS

139

LEMON TASTE TEST

INGREDIENTS

- Several lemons
- For other taste-tests try
    - Limes
    - Oranges
    - Kiwi fruit
    - Strawberries
    - Pineapple

BASIC RECIPE

Wash the lemon. Cut it into very small wedges. Put the wedges on a plate. Put the plate on a table. Hand each child a wedge and let him eat it. *(If necessary, remind the children not to eat the rind.)*

Prepare the other fruits in the same way

- Wash.
- Peel, cut, etc.
- Put on a plate.
- Serve.

Having a LEMON AND/OR LIME TASTE TEST With Children
(Remember to have the "cooks" wash their hands.)

- **Lemons**: Give each child a lemon wedge. Let him eat the fruit. Remember some will like it and others will not. Have a full-length mirror nearby. Encourage the children to look at their faces. The sour taste is making them pucker-up. *(You may want to have a camera handy. Post the photographs for all to see. Encourage parents to enjoy them too.)*

- **Limes:** Let the children wash the limes. Talk about how they are a green fruit. You may want to have lemons too. Lemons are a yellow fruit. Wedge the limes and lemons into small pieces. Hand each child a lime and let him taste it. *Good?* Hand each child a lemon. Taste it. *Does it taste like the lime? Which do they like better?*

Having a STRAWBERRY OR PINEAPPLE TASTE TEST
(Remember to have the "cooks" wash their hands.)

■ **Strawberries:** Let the children wash the strawberries and hand them to you. When they give them to you, cut off the green top. *Give the child the top and have her smell it. Feel it.* Throw the tops away. Cut the strawberries in pieces. *Let the children taste them.* Have the children look at their hands when they are finished. *Is there red juice on their fingers?*

■ **Pineapple:** Put the whole pineapple on the table. Let the children touch the outside and top. *How does it feel?* Carefully cut the top and rind off the pineapple. Hold it so each child can smell it. Cut up the pineapple into bite-size pieces. Let each child have one right away. *How does it taste?* Cut more and let the children finish the pineapple.

Having a KIWI, GRAPEFRUIT, ORANGE TASTE TEST
(Remember to have the "cooks" wash their hands.)

■ **Kiwi:** Pass the kiwi around so the children can feel the skin. Encourage them to rub it slowly and gently. *How do the kiwi feel? Soft? Furry?* Pass them back to you. Carefully peel the skins off them. Cut the fruit into slices. Put several on a plate and show the children the inside. *What do they see?* Cut the slices in quarters and let the children taste kiwi. *Who likes it? Who doesn't? How does it feel in their mouths?*

■ **Grapefruit - Oranges:** Show both fruits to the children. *Which one looks larger?* Pass them around so the children can feel the rinds. *Are they bumpy? Smooth?* Cut the fruits into small wedges. Let the children taste the grapefruit. *How does it taste? Does it make their face wrinkle up like the limes and lemons?* Now taste the oranges. *How do they taste?*

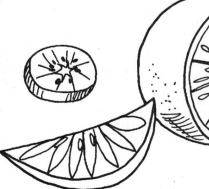

**F
O
O
D
S**

141

SNAP THE BEANS

INGREDIENTS

- Fresh green beans
- Fresh yellow beans

BASIC RECIPE

Wash the beans. Snap off the ends of each bean. Snap them in small pieces. Cook the beans in a little water or in the microwave. Drain. Put them on a plate and cover them until snack.

SNAP THE BEANS With Children
(Remember to have the "cooks" wash their hands.)

- Have the green beans in one tub of clean water and the yellow beans in another tub. Let the children wash the beans. *How do the beans feel? Hard? Soft? Look for long ones. Short ones?*

- Take the beans out of the tubs and put them on the table. Sit with the children and snap the ends off the beans. *Can they hear the beans snap?* After you have snapped the ends off each one, hand it to a child. Have her snap it into several pieces. *Sh! Can the children hear the beans snap?* Put the beans in the pan.

- After the beans have cooked, serve them to the children. *How do they taste? Do they crunch in the children's mouths? Do they feel hard in their mouths? Soft?*

QUICK COOKIES

INGREDIENTS

- Cookie mix
- Additional ingredients specified by the recipe on the box

BASIC RECIPE

Pour the cookie mix into a large bowl. Follow the recipe on the box. Spoon small cookies onto a cookie sheet and bake. Let the cookies cool. Put them on several plates and cover until snack time.

Making QUICK COOKIES With Children
(Remember to have the "cooks" wash their hands.)

- Let the children pour the cookie mix into a large bowl. *Smell good?*

- Add the other ingredients to the bowl. Give a whisk to a child and put the bowl in front of him on the table. Let him stir the mixture. Pass the bowl to another child, and let her continue to stir. *Can they smell the dough?* Continue until the dough is mixed and all the "cooks" have had an opportunity to stir.

- Give a child a small spoon. Let her spoon a little dough onto the cookie sheet. Continue until all the cookies are made. Bake. *Can you smell them?*

- After the cookies have cooled, have them for snack with a glass of milk. *How do they taste?* Smell them. *Do they smell like the dough did?*

F
O
O
D
S

143

SHAPE COOKIES

INGREDIENTS

- Refrigerated pie crust
- Simple cookie cutters

BASIC RECIPE

Roll out the pie crust. Using cookie cutters, cut the dough into shapes. Put each shape on a cookie sheet. Sprinkle the cookies with a little cinnamon. Bake as directed on the package. Let the cookies cool, put them on a plate, and cover until snack.

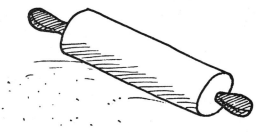

Making SHAPE COOKIES With Children
(Remember to have the "cooks" wash their hands.)

- Put a little flour on the table. Let the children spread it around. *How do their hands look? Feel?* Put the pie crust on the flour. Let the children roll it out with small rolling pins. *(Help if necessary. This could be the children's first experience with rolling out dough.)*

- Give each child a cookie cutter. Let her cut a cookie. Help her carefully pick it out and set it on the cookie sheet. Look at the "hole" in the rolled out dough. *What is it?* Continue until all the children have made cookies.

- Pass the cinnamon shaker around, and let each child shake a little cinnamon on a cookie.

- Bake. *Oh, do they smell good!*

- After the cookies have cooled, have snack. Smell the cookies again. Taste them. *Oh, do they taste good!*

COLORED MILK

INGREDIENTS

- Milk
- Food coloring
- Clear small glasses

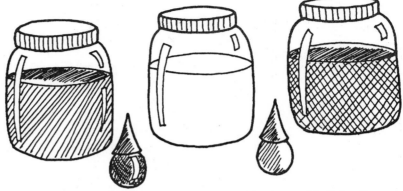

BASIC RECIPE

Pour milk in several large clear unbreakable jars with lids. Pour them about half full of milk. Bring these jars, clear glasses, and food coloring to snack. Put a different color food coloring in each jar. Shake the jars with the children. Keep one jar with white milk.

Give each child a glass. Ask him what color milk he would like to drink. Have him help you pour the color milk he chose.

Making COLORED MILK With Children
(Remember to have the "cooks" wash their hands.)

- Put the white milk, several colors of food coloring, and clear glasses on the table. Have the children look at the milk. It is white.

- Give each child a glass. Stand behind the first child and help her pour milk into her glass. Ask her what color she would like to mix in her milk. Put a drop of that color in her milk. Watch it. *What is happening?* Give her a stir stick and let her mix it. Repeat until all the children have made their own COLORED MILK. *(Remember some children may want to have white milk. That is OK.)* Look at each child's milk and name the color.

- Drink the special COLORED MILK. *How does it taste?*

FOODS

145

FUN WITH SMELLS

MAKE TOAST

YOU'LL NEED

■ Bread

■ Toaster

PREPARATION

■ Place the toaster on a table close to an electrical outlet. Tape the cord down. *(Safety)* Plug it in.

ACTIVITY

Several minutes before the children arrive, begin toasting the bread. When the children enter the school, they might get a scent of something cooking. When they enter the classroom, they will know where that great smell is coming from.

As they take off their coats, talk about what they smell. When everyone is settled, finish toasting the bread. Cut it up into small pieces and have the special treat right away.

MORE TOAST

Cinnamon Toast: Next time you enjoy this activity, have a small cinnamon shaker on the table. Let those who want to shake a little cinnamon on their toast.

SNIFF THE DOTS

YOU'LL NEED

■ Large scented stickers -- at least 2 for each child

■ Waxed paper

PREPARATION

■ Put 8-10 different scented stickers on a piece of waxed paper. Make several sheets of stickers so there are enough stickers for your children to have several during the day.

S
M
E
L
L
S

ACTIVITY

Have the stickers handy when the children come to school. During the beginning of the day walk around and show each child the stickers. Have him smell them and then give him one or let him choose one. Peel the sticker he chose off the waxed paper, and put it on his arm or the back of his hand. *(Repeat with each child.)*

During the day talk to the children about their stickers. Encourage them to put their hands to their noses and smell the stickers. *How do they smell?* If a child looses his sticker, give him another one.

SMELLING WALK

YOU'LL NEED

■ Nothing

PREPARATION

■ None

ACTIVITY

On a nice day tell the children that you are going to take them on a different kind of walk around the neighborhood -- a SMELLING WALK. Ask them to touch their noses and take a big smell. *Do they smell anything? What?* Talk. Tell them to touch their noses and take another big smell. *Do they smell anything else?* Talk. Now everyone has their noses ready and they're ready to go outside.

After everyone is outside, touch noses and smell again. *Does anyone smell anything?* Talk. Start walking as you normally might. Every once in a while stop at something - tree, mailbox, your car, flowers, fence, etc. Let the children touch their noses and smell the object. *How does it smell?* Continue on the walk. Maybe a child will see something he wants to stop and smell. Let everyone stop. Remember to touch your noses as you smell.

AIR FRESHENERS

YOU'LL NEED

- Several different hanging- type air fresheners

PREPARATION

- None

ACTIVITY

Have two of the same type of air freshener. Sit with the children on the floor. Show one freshener to them. Walk around and let each child smell it. Turn it over and let the children each smell the other side. Show them the second one. Let them smell that one also. *Do the two fresheners smell the same?*

Give the fresheners to two children. Have them rub their hands on it. Pass the fresheners to others and have them rub their hands on it. After the children have rubbed their hands, have them smell their hands. *Do they smell like the fresheners?*

Take the fresheners. Tell the children that you are going to hang them in the room, one by the cubbies for the children to smell when they take their coats on and off, and one by the bathroom door to smell when they go in and out of the bathroom.

S
M
E
L
L
S

I STUCK MY HEAD IN A LITTLE SKUNK'S HOLE

YOU'LL NEED

■ Skunk stick puppet

PREPARATION

■ Duplicate the pattern on the next page and make a skunk stick puppet. *(Use a tongue depressor or paint stir stick for the handle.)*

ACTIVITY

Sit on the floor with the children. Put the skunk puppet behind your back. Start saying the rhyme. When the skunk starts talking, bring him out so the children can see him. Encourage the children to say the repetitive line, *"Take it out . . . "* with you. *(Do this activity often. The children will soon chime in automatically.)*

I STUCK MY HEAD IN A LITTLE SKUNK'S HOLE

I stuck my head in a little skunk's hole,
And the little skunk said, *"Why bless my soul,
Take it out. Take it out. Take it out.
Remove it."*

Well, I didn't take it out, and the little skunk said,
*"You better take it out or you'll wish you had.
Take it out. Take it out. Take it out.
Sh-h-h-h! "* I removed it. Too late.

SKUNK PATTERN

SMELLS

SMELL THE FLOWERS

YOU'LL NEED

■ Fresh flowers or a flowering plant such as roses, lilacs, etc.

PREPARATION

■ Put the fresh flowers in a vase.

ACTIVITY

Have the fresh flowers or a flowering plant on the snack table. Hold the flowers, and as the children come to snack, have them each smell the flowers. After the last child has sat down, set the flowers in the middle of the table. During snack let the children smell the flowers again if they want.

After snack leave the flowers on the table or move them to a low shelf. Encourage the children to smell them throughout the day.

SMELLING GOOD

YOU'LL NEED

- Perfume

PREPARATION

- If appropriate, write a note home to your families and tell them about this activity before you do it with the children. Sometimes families like to know beforehand that you are using perfume, after-shave lotion, or skin cream with their children.

- Check your allergy list.

ACTIVITY

Have a small bottle of your favorite perfume in your pocket. Just before the children come to school, spray a little on your wrist. When the children arrive, let those who want to smell your wrist. *How do they like your perfume?*

Just before you go outside to play, ask each child if he would like you to spray a little perfume on his wrist. If he says *"yes"* spray a little; if he says, *"no"* don't do it. While you are outside, talk with the children about how their perfume smells.

Other Times: Instead of using perfume, use after-shave lotion or skin cream. *How do they smell?*

S
M
E
L
L
S

155

SOAP SCRIBBLING

YOU'LL NEED

- Lots of small bars of soap
- Dark butcher paper

PREPARATION

- Have the children help you unwrap the bars of soap. Smell them as you do. Put them in a tub.

ACTIVITY

Tape a large sheet of butcher paper to the art table. Put the bars of soap on the paper. Let the children color the paper with the soap. As they are coloring, have them smell the bars of soap and the marks they make on the paper.

Other Times: Instead of taping the paper to the art table, tape it:

- To the back of a cabinet.
- Low on a wall.
- Low on a door.
- On the floor in a less traveled area of the room.
- To the bottom of the water table. Let the children color the sides of the water table also. They can also help you sponge it clean.

SCENTED EASEL PAINT

YOU'LL NEED

- Easel paper

- Tempera paint

- Different scents, such as
  - \> Extracts
    - Vanilla
    - Peppermint
    - Spearmint
    - Wintergreen
  - \> Spices
    - Cinnamon
    - Clove
    - Pumpkin
  - \> Lemon juice
  - \> Unsweetened, powdered drink mixes
  - \> Unsweetened gelatins
  - \> Baby powder/talcum powder

S M E L L S

PREPARATION

- Make SCENTED PAINT just before the children arrive. This will insure that the scent is still strong. It will be fun and inviting for the children to smell as they come into the room.

  1. Pour the paint into a pitcher.

  2. Sprinkle in one dry or liquid scent.

  3. Mix the scent and paint. Add more scent if necessary.

  4. Store the scented paint in your easel containers and cover them immediately.

ACTIVITY

When the children arrive, have the scented paint nearby. Uncover it and let the children smell it. Tell them that it will be at the easel all day. Put it in the easel tray. Encourage the children to smell it as they paint.

SMELLY FINGER PAINTING

YOU'LL NEED

■ Scented shaving cream *(Try different scents each time you offer this activity.)*

PREPARATION

■ Empty the water table so that it is ready to use for finger painting with shaving cream.

ACTIVITY

When a child wants to finger paint with the shaving cream, have him push up his sleeves and put on a smock. Squirt a little shaving cream onto one of his hands. Ask him to hold it close to his nose and smell.

After he's smelled it, squirt a big mound in his hand and let him use it to finger paint in the water table for as long as he would like. *(Give him more if necessary.)* When he's finished, let him wipe off his hands. Have him smell his hands one more time. *Do they smell like shaving cream?*

MORE SMELLY FINGER PAINTING

Scented Finger Paints: Instead of using scented shaving cream, add cinnamon, peppermint, wintergreen, vanilla, or nutmeg to commercial finger paint. Let the children finger paint right on the art table. *(Change the scent each time you set up this activity.)*

SCENTED MARKER FUN

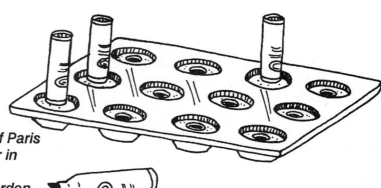

YOU'LL NEED

- Light-colored butcher paper
- Scented markers
- A marker storage tray (*Mix Plaster of Paris to the consistency of cake mix. Pour in muffin cups. Put one marker cap upside-down in each muffin cap. Harden. Add markers.*)

PREPARATION

- None

ACTIVITY

Tape a large sheet of paper to the table before the children arrive. Set the tray of markers on the table.

Let the children put on smocks and color with the scented markers. Encourage them to smell their markers and their friend's markers as they color. After a while suggest they trade markers with the person next to them. Let each child color for as long as he would like.

Another Time: Tape a large piece of white cardboard to the table and let the children color it.

Mmm! Grape!

SMELLS

159

BUILDING BLOCKS Library

The Circle Time Series

by Liz and Dick Wilmes. Hundreds of activities for large and small groups of children. Each book is filled with Language and Active games, Fingerplays, Songs, Stories, Snacks, and more. A great resource for every library shelf.

Circle Time Book
Captures the spirit of 39 holidays and seasons.
ISBN 0-943452-00-7   **$ 12.95**

Everyday Circle Times
Over 900 ideas. Choose from 48 topics divided into 7 sections: self-concept, basic concepts, animals, foods, science, occupations, and recreation.
ISBN 0-943452-01-5   **$16.95**

More Everyday Circle Times
Divided into the same 7 sections as EVERYDAY. Features new topics such as Birds and Pizza, plus all new ideas for some popular topics contained in EVERYDAY.
ISBN 0-943452-14-7   **$16.95**

Yearful of Circle Times
52 different topics to use weekly, by seasons, or mixed throughout the year. New Friends, Signs of Fall, Snowfolk Fun, and much more.
ISBN 0-943452-10-4   **$16.95**

Paint Without Brushes

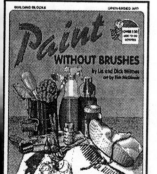

by Liz and Dick Wilmes. Use common materials which you already have. Discover the painting possibilities in your classroom! PAINT WITHOUT BRUSHES gives your children open-ended art activities to explore paint in lots of creative ways. A valuable art resource. One you'll want to use daily.
ISBN 0-943452-15-5   **$12.95**

Easel Art

by Liz & Dick Wilmes. Let the children use easels, walls, outside fences, clip boards, and more as they enjoy the variety of art activities filling the pages of EASEL ART. A great book to expand young children's art experiences.
ISBN 0-943452-25-2   **$ 12.95**

Everyday Bulletin Boards

by Wilmes and Moehling. Features borders, murals, backgrounds, and other open-ended art to display on your bulletin boards. Plus board ideas with patterns, which teachers can make and use to enhance their curriculum.
ISBN 0-943452-09-0   **$ 12.95**

Exploring Art

by Liz and Dick Wilmes. EXPLORING ART is divided by months. Over 250 art ideas for paint, chalk, doughs, scissors, and more. Easy to set-up in your classroom.
ISBN 0-943452-05-8   **$19.95**

CIRCLE TIME

ART

LEARNING GAMES & ACTIVITIES

Magnet Board Fun

by Liz and Dick Wilmes. Every classroom has a magnet board, every home a refrigerator. MAGNET BOARD FUN is crammed full of games, songs, and stories for your home and classroom. Hundreds of patterns to reproduce, color, and use immediately.
ISBN 0-943452-28-7   **$16.95**

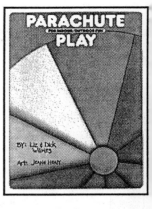

Parachute Play

by Liz and Dick Wilmes. A year 'round approach to one of the most versatile pieces of large muscle equipment. Starting with basic techniques, PARACHUTE PLAY provides over 100 activities to use with your parachute.
ISBN 0-943452-03-1   **$ 9.95**

Activities Unlimited

by Adler, Caton, and Cleveland. Hundreds of innovative activities to help your children develop fine and gross motor skills, increase their language, become self-reliant, and play cooperatively. Whether you're a beginning teacher or a veteran, this book will quickly become one of your favorites.
ISBN 0-943452-17-1   **$16.95**

Felt Board Fingerplays

by Liz and Dick Wilmes. Over fifty popular fingerplays, each with full-size patterns. All accompanied by games and activities. Divided by seasons, this book is a quick reference for a year full of fingerplay fun.
ISBN 0-943452-26-0   **$16.95**

Felt Board Fun

by Liz and Dick Wilmes. Make your felt board come alive. Discover how versatile it is as the children become involved with a wide range of activities. This unique book has over 150 ideas with accompanying patterns.
ISBN 0-943452-02-3   **$16.95**

Table & Floor Games

by Liz and Dick Wilmes. 32 easy-to-make, fun-to-play table/floor games with accompanying patterns ready to trace or photocopy. Teach beginning concepts such as matching, counting, colors, alphabet, sorting and so on.
ISBN 0-943452-16-3   **$19.95**

Learning Centers

by Liz and Dick Wilmes. Hundreds of open-ended activities to quickly involve and excite your children. You'll use it every time you plan and whenever you need a quick, additional activity. A must for every teacher's bookshelf.
ISBN 0-943452-13-9   **$19.95**

Play With Big Boxes

by Liz and Dick Wilmes. Children love big boxes. Turn them into boats, telephone booths, tents, and other play areas. Bring them to art and let children collage, build, and paint them. Use them in learning centers for games, play stages, quiet spaces, puzzles, and more, more, more.
ISBN 0-943452-23-6   **$ 12.95**

Play With Small Boxes

by Liz and Dick Wilmes. Small boxes are free, fun, and provide unlimited possibilities. Use them for telephones, skates, scoops, pails, beds, buggies, and more. So many easy activities, you'll want to use small boxes every day.
ISBN 0-943452-24-4   **$ 12.95**

2's Experience Series

by Liz and Dick Wilmes. An exciting series developed especially for toddlers and twos!

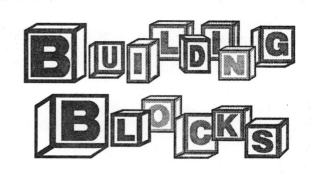

2's Experience – Art
Scribble, Paint, Smear, Mix , Tear, Mold, Taste, and more. Over 150 activities, plus lots of recipes and hints.
ISBN 0-943452-21-X   **$16.95**

2's Experience – Dramatic Play
Dress up and pretend! Hundreds of imaginary characters... fire-fighters, campers, bus drivers, and more.
ISBN 0-943452-20-1   **$12.95**

2's Experience – Felt Board Fun
Make your felt board come alive. Enjoy stories, activities, and rhymes developed just for very young children. Hundreds of extra large patterns feature teddy bears, birthdays, farm animals, and much, much more.
ISBN 0-943452-19-8   **$14.95**

2's Experience – Fingerplays
A wonderful collection of easy fingerplays with accompanying games and large FINGERPLAY CARDS.
ISBN 0-943452-18-X   **$12.95**

2's Experience – Sensory Play
Hundreds of playful, multi-sensory activities to encourage children to look, listen, taste, touch, and smell.
ISBN 0-943452-22-8   **$14.95**

T O D D L E R S & T W O ' S

BUILDING BLOCKS Subscription	**$20.00**
2's EXPERIENCE Series	
2'S EXPERIENCE - ART	16.95
2'S EXPERIENCE - DRAMATIC PLAY	12.95
2'S EXPERIENCE - FELTBOARD FUN	14.95
2'S EXPERIENCE - FINGERPLAYS	12.95
2'S EXPERIENCE - SENSORY PLAY	14.95
CIRCLE TIME Series	
CIRCLE TIME BOOK	12.95
EVERYDAY CIRCLE TIMES	16.95
MORE EVERYDAY CIRCLE TIMES	16.95
YEARFUL OF CIRCLE TIMES	16.95
ART	
EASEL ART	12.95
EVERYDAY BULLETIN BOARDS	12.95
EXPLORING ART	19.95
PAINT WITHOUT BRUSHES	12.95
LEARNING GAMES & ACTIVITIES	
ACTIVITIES UNLIMITED	16.95
FELT BOARD FINGERPLAYS	16.95
FELT BOARD FUN	16.95
LEARNING CENTERS	19.95
MAGNET BOARD FUN	16.95
PARACHUTE PLAY	9.95
PLAY WITH BIG BOXES	12.95
PLAY WITH SMALL BOXES	12.95
TABLE & FLOOR GAMES	19.95

Prices subject to change without notice.

All books available from full-service book stores, educational stores, and school supply catalogs.